Fred Billington

(August 2008)

"A Large Meat Eater"

by

Tony Joseph

Bunthorne Books

Bristol

2008

D'Oyly Carte Personalities Series

1: Frederick Neebe
2: Charles Goulding
3: Aileen Davies
4: Evelyn Gardiner
5: Emmie Owen and Florence Perry
6: Leonard Osborn
7: Fred Billington

ISBN: 978-0-9507992-9-2

Published by:
Bunthorne Books
105 Bartholomews Square
Bristol
BS7 OQB

Printed by:
4word Ltd
Unit 15
Baker's Park
Cater Road
Bristol
BS13 7TT

Contents

Fred Billington as Pooh-Bah, New York, 1885
(Collection: David Stone)

Introduction

"Off the stage he was as jovial as on it, and upheld his position as 'Father' and Pooh-Bah of the Company in all emergencies."
(From Billington's obituary in the *Daily Mail*)

Why Fred Billington?

Life is strange. Fred Billington had not been on my list of potential subjects for this series of D'Oyly Carte personalities at all. And he would probably have stayed that way had it not been for an email I received from a longstanding G&S friend, Michael Symes, shortly after the publication of my previous book on Leonard Osborn. "I hope one day," wrote Michael very simply, "you will turn your attention to Fred Billington," and left me to ponder the idea in my own time.

As I said, life is strange. My immediate reaction to the idea was a definite "no". Fred Billington – yes, he was an interesting thought. But as a subject for a biography he was not for me.

That was before lunch.

Lunch over, I went out for the first part of the afternoon, and while I was out I found myself mentally drafting Michael a reply, explaining why I was turning his suggestion down. But ... by that same evening I'd had a complete change of mind, and had decided Fred Billington would make a splendid subject after all.

So – next question. Why had my initial reaction to making him one of my subjects been so uncompromisingly negative? There were two reasons.

The first of those reasons, and the easier to explain, had to do with the limited scope of his career. Billington joined D'Oyly Carte in 1879 at the age of twenty-five; and apart from one scarcely noticeable short break he remained with the Company, performing primarily in Gilbert and Sullivan, for no fewer than thirty-eight years, right up to his death in 1917.

During those years he played eighteen G&S parts – a considerable number, even though some way from a record – the majority of them what for convenience may be called the heavy comedian "Pooh-Bah" parts. And by the time he was halfway through his career he had come to be regarded by vast numbers of people as the perfect interpreter of those parts. But (I thought) how much can you say about the performances of a man whose career consisted of playing basically the same parts in the same productions year after year after year?

To take just two examples of those parts. He played Pooh-Bah for the first time in 1885 when he was coming up to thirty-one, and he was still playing Pooh-Bah over thirty years later when he was in his sixties. Similarly he played Wilfred Shadbolt for the first time in 1889 when he was coming up to thirty-four and was still playing that part in his sixties too.

Now, obviously, an actor playing any part in his sixties won't be playing it in quite the same way as he played it in his thirties. Assuming he's an intelligent performer, thirty years will have helped him fine-tune it if nothing else. But the difference between the two portrayals will most likely be no more than in matters of detail; and this would have been especially the case where Fred Billington was concerned. With him, after all, we're talking entirely about the D'Oyly Carte productions, which in essence remained unchanged throughout his time in the Company and for decades afterwards.

In consequence, it seemed to me likely that all that would need to be said about his performances could be fitted into a single chapter. There would presumably be something to say about his early life, as well as his life offstage while in the Company, that might fill another chapter or two.

But there could be nothing to be said about his time after leaving D'Oyly Carte because he never left it. Likewise I was doubtful whether there'd be anything to say about his private life in the sense of family or sexual relationships, because I'd ascertained previously that he didn't have any significant relationships in either category. And taken altogether, these various considerations hardly seemed sufficient to form the basis for a biography of any length or depth.

My second reason for not wanting to tackle him is much harder to explain – or, at least, harder to explain without giving the wrong impression. It had to do with his origin and background, and may be best summed up like this:

Fred Billington was a Yorkshireman, born near Huddersfield. From what I thought I knew about him already, he appeared to have been the very model of what the rest of the country thinks of as a Yorkshireman – that is, someone blunt, bluff and down-to-earth; someone with no time for sentimentality; someone liable to be bloody-minded; someone who was never afraid to say what he thought. "He had Yorkshire written all over him," as one acquaintance obligingly put it.

There were, of course, a fair number of other Yorkshiremen in D'Oyly Carte down the years, but none of those others seem to have embodied the outsider's view of a Yorkshireman in quite the way he did. To understand and appreciate him fully, therefore, shouldn't his biography be written by a Yorkshireman, or at any rate by a northerner? How could someone like myself who has always lived in the South; who has always thought of himself as a southerner; and who has never – if he's honest – been totally at ease with the blunt, bluff, down-to-earth characters of this world … how could I write a biography of someone with whom I felt no obvious affinity?

So what led me to change my mind and decide Fred Billington was a good subject to write about after all? There were three factors. And the first of those factors concerned the particular period of his time in D'Oyly Carte and, more specifically, the second half of that period. Taking the people I'd made the subjects of previous books in this series, I'd had a representative or representatives from each D'Oyly Carte decade with the exception of the first two decades of the twentieth century (1900-1919) and, much later, the 1960s and early 1970s. Adding Fred Billington to their number would give me a representative of those two early decades and so fill one of my gaps.

The second factor that made me change my mind about him related to the parts he played – that is, Pooh-Bah *et al*. I'd been wanting for some time to tackle one of the D'Oyly Carte performers who played those parts. But the question had always previously been "which of them?" What about one of those I'd seen play one or more of the parts on stage myself? There were five of these: Richard Walker, Richard Watson, Fisher Morgan, Arthur Richards and Kenneth Sandford. Surely one of those five was the answer? But unfortunately it wasn't. None of those five – and this is to my detriment, not theirs – had quite gripped me enough to make me say "Yes, he was the perfect Pooh-Bah, or the perfect Shadbolt, or the perfect Don Alhambra. He's the one for me now."

Why was that? I can give the answer by citing the name of another performer: Leo Sheffield.

Leo Sheffield was Fred Billington's D'Oyly Carte successor, and his name will reappear later in this book. And despite the fact that I never saw him on stage – he'd left the Company well before I was born – despite the fact that my appreciation of him had come solely from hearing his voice on record – I'd always felt *he* was the man who must have been the perfect Pooh-Bah, the perfect Don Alhambra, Sergeant of Police and so on; the man who gave those parts an extra "something" that none of his successors, whatever their merits, managed to give in the same way.

What was that "something"? I think the answer here is the tremendous sense of enjoyment – a sort of bubbling undercurrent of delight – in what he was doing that came across in every part he played. I have only to put on one of his recordings and hear him sing a couple of bars to be conscious of my face creasing into a smile; and there is ample evidence to suggest that he'd only to make his entrance on stage to have the faces of his audiences creasing likewise. He was hugely popular – hugely popular and greatly loved.

So Leo Sheffield was, for me, the performer against whom I have judged every performer who followed him in those roles; and I don't totally discount the possibility of making him the subject of a biography at some time in the future. Yet partly because I had already written biographies of two other performers (Charles Goulding and Aileen Davies) whose time in the Company coincided with the time when his popularity reached its height – the 1920s – I have shied away from doing so just yet.

But even if I didn't go for Sheffield there was, I could now see, the perfect substitute – the perfect Lord High Substitute in fact – ready to hand: Fred Billington.

Billington, unfortunately, made no recordings, so what his voice was like can only be guessed at. But in terms of his performances as a whole I'd already got the impression that he radiated a sense of enjoyment in what he was doing similar to that radiated by Sheffield himself. I'd gathered too that he was as popular with his audiences, and almost as much loved by them, as the latter was to be.

I'd also gathered – and this was the third factor that made me decide he would make a good biographical subject – that he was a "character". And "characters", as I became particularly aware when I was working on a biography of the contralto Evelyn Gardiner, are great fun to write about. Moreover I knew enough to realise that not only was he a character but that he became, in the later part of his life, what would nowadays be called a national treasure. Unlike Sir Joseph Porter when considering whether or not to reject Josephine in Act Two of *HMS Pinafore* (I happily told myself) he'd "do".

Yes, but … what of the initial reservations I'd had about doing him? What of my concern about the limited scope of his career? What of my concern, as an effete, soft-centred and anything but blunt southerner, presuming to write the biography of a blunt no-nonsense Yorkshireman? I decided quite simply that those concerns could be coped with if and when the need to cope with them arose.

Furthermore on the second count – the southerner/Yorkshireman aspect – I could point to an interesting and encouraging precedent. Entirely by chance I had just been reading a biography of the one-time Yorkshire cricketer Geoffrey Boycott. It was a biography written by a journalist, Leo McKinstry. A previous biographer of Boycott, explained McKinstry, had written that "only a Yorkshireman" could properly comprehend the Boycott story in terms of "its unique place in the history of English cricket". But McKinstry was having none of that. In the preface to his own book he wrote:

> "If that were true then I, as an Ulsterman living in Essex, have laboured in vain. Yet I believe that this robust view has been part of the problem of interpreting the Boycott phenomenon. By focusing narrowly on Yorkshire, such an approach ignores the truth that Boycott has always been much more than [a] Yorkshire cricketer."

Swap the name Billington for Boycott and the phrase "Yorkshire actor-singer" for "Yorkshire cricketer" and there you have it.

As when I was working on each of my previous books, there are a number of people I particularly want to thank for their help and encouragement while I've been engaged on this present one; and they are: Katie Barnes; Peter Brading; Lorna Brooks, Sarah Harding, Carol Hardy and Pam Riding of Huddersfield Public Library; Christopher I. Browne; Geoffrey Dixon; Jo Elsworth and Bex Carrington of the University of Bristol Theatre Collection; Mary Gilhooly, the D'Oyly Carte Archivist; Tony Gower, who once again helped prepare the illustrations; Bruce Graham, a Pooh-Bah of our own time; Rachel Hassall; Brian Jones; George Low; Simon Moss; Roderick Murray; David Stone; Selwyn Tillett; and Penny Woodruff.

I should also like to thank Claire Hudson of the V&A Theatre Collections for permission to reproduce letters in the collections written by Helen and Richard D'Oyly Carte.

I am grateful to Leo McKinstry for permission to quote the extract from his biography of Geoffrey Boycott (*Boycs: the true story*) published by Partridge in 2000; and to Joanne Fitton of Bury Museum and Archives for permission to reproduce the photograph of Bury's Royal Hotel (image reference b12456) on page 34.

Permission to reproduce letters, photographs and other material relating to Fred Billington is given by the D'Oyly Carte Opera Trust Ltd. Copyright is protected, and these materials may not be reproduced in any medium without permission of the D'Oyly Carte Opera Trust Ltd. This includes permission to reproduce the letters written by Helen and Richard D'Oyly Carte referred to above.

Finally I should like to thank Gordon Young, Steve Drew, John Roost and Dave Vinson of *4word Ltd*, my printers, for their part in bringing this book to fruition; and Joy for, as it says in the thesaurus, "advice, aid, assistance, co-operation, guidance and help".

Tony Joseph

Fred Billington: the best known photograph
(Collection: Katie Barnes)

"He *is* a Yorkshireman", 1854-79

"I am just a plain Yorkshireman and don't ever wish to be considered anything else."

(Billington to an interviewer, 1913)

The scene was the golf course at Hoylake in Cheshire. The sun was shining, the birds were singing, and Fred Billington was about to play a round against a local clergyman, a Reverend Atkinson. Just before the two of them got started, Billington said abruptly:

"I should warn you, lad, I talk to my ball at each hole to make sure it knows what's expected of it."

The clergyman laughed a little nervously.

"That's all right," he replied. "There's a lot of, er, human nature in this game."

They teed off. All went well for the first few holes. But then, at the next hole, the clergyman played a shot that went disastrously awry. The ball landed among some railway sleepers. The reverend gentleman made several vicious jabs at it to try to free it and, in the process, broke his favourite club. In sheer exasperation he exclaimed:

"Oh – Buttons!" Then "Buttons – Buttons – BUTTONS!"

Billington looked at him in equal exasperation.

"Buttons be damned!" he said. "Why don't you say …?" and out came a stream of vivid expletives.

The clergyman looked at him in turn, momentarily shocked, then suddenly broke into a smile.

"Thank you so much, Mr Billington," he said in a tone of intense relief.

Two letters:

60 Grafton Street
Oxford Road
Manchester

May 6th 1894

"My dear Hutton

Many thanks for yours. Delighted to have dinner with you and Mrs Hutton at the Queen's [Hotel] next Friday.

Six o'clock will suit me first rate, but let me know if any other time between five and seven will be more convenient for you …

Yours very truly
Fred Billington."

60 Grafton Street [etc]
May 8th 1894

"Dear Hutton

Thanks for yours. Very sorry Mrs Hutton won't be able to turn up on Friday night. Suppose, under the circumstances, we 'cry off' as regards the dinner and, instead, you come round to my dressing room after the first act of *Pirates* and we'll have a jaw and a drink – you'll have fifteen minutes interval. Let it stand at this, old chap.

Yours very truly [*again*]
Fred Billington."

Golf – colourful language – a hotel – dinner – having a jaw. Welcome to the world of Fred Billington!

Fred Billington was born on July 1st 1854, the third of four sons of Thomas Billington and his wife Sarah, born Sarah Drake.

For the record it must be mentioned straight away that his first name, strictly speaking, was Frederick. But as far as I can make out he was always known simply as Fred, always signed himself (as on those two letters above) "Fred". Accordingly Fred is the name I've used for him throughout this book.

And while we're on names, it also seems appropriate to mention straight away that he acquired at some point the fairly obvious nickname of Billy. "Billy" was the name by which he would be known, eventually, to most of his D'Oyly Carte colleagues.

His place of birth is sometimes given as Huddersfield, and Huddersfield may more or less fairly be considered his home town. But he actually came into the world in Lockwood, a mile and a half to the south. Lockwood was then a separate township, with a population of five and a half thousand, though it was not to be a separate township much longer, becoming part of Huddersfield in 1868.

It was, though, a place of charm and character. Brian Clarke, a local man who has written its history, incorporates on his title-page a description of its charm penned back in 1830 that makes it sound, at least at that time, like a rural idyll:

"The village of Lockwood is beautifully and delightfully situated in the valley of the Holne, and lies in a romantic and finely-sheltered country. As a summer retreat Lockwood cannot be surpassed."

And even allowing for the beginnings and growth of industrialisation that had occurred by the time Fred Billington came along, it was clearly not a bad place for a boy to spend his childhood.

Thomas and Sarah Billington had got married in 1844, when Thomas was twenty-four and Sarah nineteen. Sarah came from Honley, a village two miles to the south. But Thomas was born in Huddersfield itself, and while they may possibly have started their married life elsewhere, they were established in Lockwood by 1851, a year when a new census was taken. By 1851, also, their first two sons had been born: Joseph, who was by then aged four, and George, aged just one. Finally, following Fred's arrival, came Walter, born in 1856.

At the time of Fred's birth the family were living in Spa Terrace, a short street of back-to-back houses that no longer exist. Lockwood's economy, like that of Huddersfield itself and most of the surrounding area, was based on a thriving wool and cloth trade, and Thomas Billington was one of many thousands of local people employed in the woollen industry. He was variously described in census and other records as a cloth dresser, a woollen cloth finisher, an overlooker of woollen machinery and – indicating an ability to work with figures – a book-keeper. In due course two of his sons, Joseph (as a warehouse boy) and Walter went into the woollen industry as well.

But what of the other two? What of George – and what of Fred? It was the Victorian era; and George, it seems likely, was one of the legion of Victorian children who died young - died, that is, before he was old enough to work in wool or anything else; while for some reason Fred never got caught up – at least in terms of manual work – in the woollen or other cloth industry at all. Instead, as it was put in one of the many press interviews he was eventually to give, he was "intended for commercial pursuits".

He seems to have inherited his father's ability with figures. For having left school – Lockwood National School, which had opened the year before he was born – he first went to work in the office of Messrs Austin and Bennett, a firm of Huddersfield accountants. Later he was employed in the Huddersfield Post Office, the Huddersfield Corporation offices and, according to one somewhat doubtful source, the Huddersfield Water Board.

This took things to 1874, when he was twenty. That year the Huddersfield Chief Clerk, a man named George Harrison, was appointed Borough Accountant of Stockton-on-Tees outside Yorkshire in County Durham. At much the same time, possibly at Harrison's instigation, Billington was appointed to a clerical position in the administrative offices of the same town, and went off to work there at the end of that year or early the next year, 1875.

A view of Lockwood as it is today
(Photograph: Bruce Graham)

Was he happy? Happy, that is, as a clerk, happy in a desk job? Even though not physically demanding in the way a mill or factory job would have been, the work could well have been monotonous and the hours were almost certainly long. So, no, he wasn't happy. As he forcefully, many years later, told another press interviewer:

"I loathed work. I think that anybody who needn't work, and does, is an adjectival fool."

Welcome again to the world of Fred Billington!

But if work – or at any rate work that meant being shut in an office all day – didn't suit him, what might suit him better? The answer that suggested itself was ... some sort of performing.

The urge to perform was an urge that had been with him from his early days. So how and where did he start? The answer here – as it would be with any number of other D'Oyly Carte performers down the years – was in church. As he explained:

"I was in a church choir at Lockwood for many years, singing treble, alto, tenor, bass, just as my voice wobbled, while I was growing from boyhood up to the age of twenty-one."

The church was Lockwood Emmanuel, the town's parish church, built between 1828 and 1830 from government funds made available for the building of many new churches as a way of giving thanks to God for the British victory, several years earlier, over Napoleon. Then when Billington moved to Stockton he sang not only in the parish (Anglican) church but in the town's Roman Catholic church too, as well as with the Stockton Choral Society. Clearly it caused him no problem being associated with the activities of more than one religious denomination; and as a way of gaining the experience needed to become a professional singer all this was invaluable.

He had also, though in a lesser way, tried acting, becoming for a time a member of a local amateur dramatic society. But his acting experience was still fairly limited when, sometime during the summer of 1879, the year he became twenty-five, he made a momentous decision.

He, this archetypal Yorkshireman, decided to turn his back on Yorkshire and the North-East and try his luck as a singer and actor in London.

How can we picture him as, like a Victorian Dick Whittington (travelling of course by train rather than trudging the distance on foot, and without Whittington's proverbial cat in tow) he made his way to the great metropolis?

There is, unfortunately, little specific evidence to go on in this respect, as there are no photographs of him dating from this early stage of his life. Nonetheless it can definitely be said that he was fairly tall (five foot nine) and that he had brown hair and brown eyes. It can also, I think, be said with reasonable certainty that he looked older than he was – middle-aged, even; and that he was unlikely to have been the slimmest young-cum-middle-aged person who ever alighted from a train at a London terminus.

But how did London receive him? London, to the provincial newcomer, can easily appear unwelcoming, especially if that newcomer is looking for work and has no contacts to help him find it. More than twenty-five years later Billington told an interviewer that he detested the place, and that it always reminded him of his "hard up" time. In that interview he claimed to have had "the peculiar, not to say unenviable experience of dossing two nights on the Thames Embankment and" – probably even worse – "trying the effects of total abstinence from food of any kind for three days, the finest known remedy for plumpness" – of which more anon. Whether this was the full extent of his misery, or whether there was more to it that he didn't mention is impossible to say. But it can only have lasted a few weeks at the outside, for by mid to late July he had found work of the sort he wanted.

At the Alhambra Theatre in Leicester Square, preparations were under way for a new production of a comic opera or *opera bouffe* called *The Princess of Trebizonde*, which was announced to open on July 28th. *The Princess of Trebizonde*, which had first been seen in London nine years earlier, was a piece by Offenbach. It had lively music plus "the great advantage of a plot which all can understand"; and for this production Billington managed to get himself engaged as a chorister. His professional performing career had begun.

One of the leading performers in *Trebizonde* this time round was a lady named Carrie Braham, the opera's principal contralto, who deeply impressed the reviewer covering the production for the dramatic-theatrical newspaper the *Era*:

> "Miss Carrie Braham" (wrote this gentleman) "eminently qualified by Nature to appear as 'the Strong Woman of the Wilderness', was completely successful in this Amazonian part, and we have little doubt that had the weights [*sic*] been as heavy as they were represented to be, Miss Carrie Braham could have carried them. She was full of animation and spirit. And if her form was heavy, her rendering of the character was not so but, on the contrary, was extremely sprightly."

Any similarity to any of the contralto parts to be created by Gilbert and Sullivan was of course entirely coincidental. But that said, the current production of the Offenbach work included a G&S link of its own, in that two members of the cast had actually appeared in G&S roles on their own account. One of the two was Alice May, who had played in the original production of *The Sorcerer* and had created the soprano part of Aline. The other was Furneaux Cook who had played Dr Daly in the same opera on tour.

And it was not long before the G&S link came to include Billington too. One evening some way into *Trebizonde's* run, the audience included a lady named Helen Lenoir.

Officially Helen Lenoir was secretary to Richard D'Oyly Carte, the man whose initiative and drive had brought Gilbert and Sullivan together. But the designation "secretary" came nowhere near to describing the extent and variety of her activities and responsibilities or the number of hours she put in. A businesswoman of boundless capability and a born organiser, she was someone on whom Carte came to rely to such an extent that she became all but indispensable to him – and not only for what she did in terms of organisation and financial matters.

For having previously, even if only fairly briefly, been an actress, she had as keen an instinct for things theatrical as he had himself. Those things included talent spotting. It was very likely a need to seek out new talent that had led her to the Alhambra that summer evening. And the member of the *Trebizonde* cast who immediately stood out for her as having a talent to cultivate was Fred Billington.

The precise details are lacking, but it seems she lost no time in introducing herself to him. The two got on well together from the start and, remarkably, it was the beginning of a friendship that lasted till her death more than thirty years later – "remarkably" because, apart from the fact they were much of an age and that neither of them was a Londoner, they could hardly have been more different.

He was from Yorkshire and the son of a wool worker. *She* was Scottish and the daughter of a lawyer. *She* was now in theatrical management or, to put it another way, represented an employer. *He* remained throughout his life an employee, and indeed *her* employee in D'Oyly Carte from that time on. Somehow she got the Alhambra management to release him from the production of *Trebizonde* midway through September before that production closed, in order that he could join a new D'Oyly Carte Company then being formed to present and tour *HMS Pinafore*.

Before getting properly started on Billington's D'Oyly Carte career, though, it may be as well to refer briefly to the D'Oyly Carte/G&S story itself, and where necessary to recap a little, so as to make clear where things had got to in the story when he first became part of it in that September of 1879.

The story, in fact, was then still in its early chapters, having begun less than five years previously with the production of *Trial by Jury* in March 1875. Two and a half years after that, in November 1877, had come *The Sorcerer*, and six months after *that*, in May 1878, *HMS Pinafore*. *Trial by Jury*, though only a one-act piece, had been a riotous success from the beginning. *The Sorcerer*, the first full-length D'Oyly Carte opera, had done well too, if without establishing the G&S partnership fully; and it wasn't till *HMS Pinafore* had worked through a somewhat fraught opening period and got properly into its stride that it became absolutely clear that G&S had come to stay.

Pinafore's popularity was phenomenal. Its success had enabled Carte to rid himself of the backers whose financial assistance he had initially needed to get the partnership off the ground. At the Opera Comique, the theatre just off the Strand which he had taken for this purpose, it had already passed its four hundredth performance. He was now engaged on plans to send a Company to play it in America. He already had two companies touring it in the provinces at home, and was currently in the process of getting together a third Company to do likewise. This Company, officially dubbed the Second London Company, was the Company that Fred Billington was now joining.

He could hardly have joined it at a better and more exciting time.

The new Company's opening was duly announced in the *Era*:

"National Standard Theatre, Bishopsgate. Engagement … of Mr D'Oyly Carte's Opera Company in the World-Renowned Opera by W.S. Gilbert and Arthur Sullivan, *HMS Pinafore*, with all the original effects, and produced under the direction of the author and composer.

Monday September 22nd and Every Evening at 7.30: *The Love Test*. At 8.30 *HMS Pinafore*. Characters by Messrs James A. Meade, George Temple, Fabrini, Aynsley Cook, Billington, Montelli, Fitzalmont; Mesdames Gordon, Haidee Crofton, Dundas, etc."

The paper's reviewer present on the first night, however, had certain reservations about that Company's performance. Carte had got the cast finally settled only just in time, having had "difficulties in procuring artists to represent the chief characters". The consequence was that, very unusually for a D'Oyly Carte Company, most of the performers and other people involved came to that first night insufficiently rehearsed.

For example, while

"a full chorus and an increased band … gave due effect to the choral and instrumental departments which throughout the first act went uncommonly well"

the second act needed further rehearsals "to make matters go smoothly". And likewise

"Miss Duglas Gordon has at least two requisites for the character of Josephine: a pleasing appearance on the stage and an excellent voice. Her execution of the music in the first act gained for the young lady unanimous approval. In the second [act] she will succeed better when quite familiar with the music"

which, assuming this was a fair comment, was also a pretty damning one, since Miss Gordon had actually been drafted into the Company from the first *Pinafore* touring Company, and had been singing Josephine's music for a year.

By contrast Fred Billington, who had presumably been rehearsing in the daytime while still playing in *Trebizonde* in the evenings, came in for none of these strictures. It helped, perhaps, that he made his D'Oyly Carte debut in a part that, in G&S terms, is relatively straightforward to play: Bill Bobstay, the *Pinafore* "Boatswain". In later years Bobstay came generally to be regarded as a chorister's part. But it's quite a substantial part and, whatever its limitations,

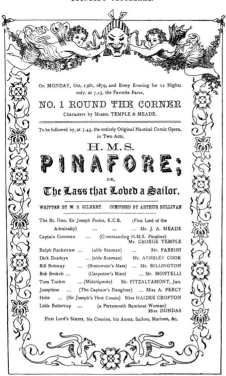

On MONDAY, Oct. 13th, 1879, and Every Evening for 12 Nights only, at 7.15, the Favorite Farce,

NO. 1 ROUND THE CORNER

Characters by Messrs. TEMPLE & MEADE.

To be followed by, at 7.45, the entirely Original Nautical Comic Opera, in Two Acts,

H. M. S.
PINAFORE;
OR,
The Lass that Loved a Sailor.

WRITTEN BY W. S. GILBERT.   COMPOSED BY ARTHUR SULLIVAN

The Rt. Hon. Sir Joseph Porter, K.C.B.	(First Lord of the Admiralty)	... Mr. J. A. MEADE
Captain Corcoran ...	(Commanding H.M.S. Pinafore)	Mr. GEORGE TEMPLE
Ralph Rackstraw ...	(able Seaman)	Mr. FABRINI
Dick Deadeye ...	(able Seaman)	Mr. AYNSLEY COOK
Bill Bobstay ...	(Boatswain's Mate)	... Mr. BILLINGTON
Bob Beckett ...	(Carpenter's Mate)	... Mr. MONTELLI
Tom Tucker ...	(Midshipmite)	Mr. FITZALTAMONT, Jun.
Josephine ...	(The Captain's Daughter)	... Miss A. PERCY
Hebe ...	(Sir Joseph's First Cousin)	Miss HAIDEE CROFTON
Little Buttercup ...	(a Portsmouth Bumboat Woman)	Miss DUNDAS

First Lord's Sisters, his Cousins, his Aunts, Sailors, Marines, &c.

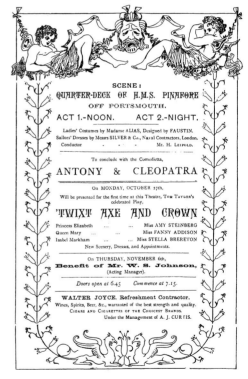

SCENE:
QUARTER-DECK OF H.M.S. PINAFORE
OFF PORTSMOUTH.
ACT 1.-NOON.   **ACT 2.-NIGHT.**

Ladies' Costumes by Madame ALIAS, Designed by FAUSTIN.
Sailors' Dresses by Messrs SILVER & Co., Naval Contractors, London.
Conductor - - - Mr. H. LEIPOLD.

To conclude with the Comedietta,

ANTONY & CLEOPATRA

On MONDAY, OCTOBER 27th,

Will be presented for the first time at this Theatre, TOM TAYLOR's celebrated Play,

'TWIXT AXE AND CROWN

Princess Elizabeth	...	... Miss AMY STEINBERG
Queen Mary	... ...	Miss FANNY ADDISON
Isabel Markham	...	... Miss STELLA BRERETON

New Scenery, Dresses, and Appointments.

On THURSDAY, NOVEMBER 6th,
Benefit of Mr. W. S. Johnson,
(Acting Manager).

Doors open at 6.45   *Commence at 7.15.*

WALTER JOYCE, Refreshment Contractor.

Wines, Spirits, Beer, &c., warranted of the best strength and quality.
CIGARS AND CIGARETTES OF THE CHOICEST BRANDS.
Under the Management of A. J. CURTIS.

Billington's first D'Oyly Carte tour: programme for *HMS Pinafore*
in Camden Town
(Collection: George Low)

it includes the singing of what had quickly become one of the most popular songs in the opera. "Mr Billington", wrote the *Era* reviewer,

> "was a manly and hearty Bill Bobstay, and his genial singing of 'He is an Englishman' led to an encore being insisted on."

After three weeks in Bishopsgate in *east* London the Company moved to *north* London for a two week season at the Royal Park Theatre in Camden Town. London theatres in those days – and for decades afterwards – could be divided into two distinct groups. On the one hand there was the cluster of "Central London" theatres in the West End, and on the other there were what might be called "local" theatres dotted around the capital elsewhere. The clientele of the Central London theatres would rarely show up at any of the "local" theatres, while the "local" theatregoers would stick firmly to their own local theatres, and that would be that – it was as though the two worlds were entirely separate. During his years in D'Oyly Carte Fred Billington was to play several seasons at these local theatres, and almost certainly he thought of them more as provincial venues than as part of that London he claimed to detest.

But now London in both its aspects could temporarily at least be forgotten. For, following their two weeks in Camden Town, the Company left the capital and headed off on a typical D'Oyly Carte tour of provincial towns and cities. Between October 27th and December 13th this tour took them in turn to Cambridge, Portsmouth, Birmingham, Dublin (Billington's first visit to Ireland), Newcastle, Chester, Shrewsbury, Hereford and Worcester.

During this tour, when they were either in Cambridge or Portsmouth, Billington was given a change of part. Having begun his D'Oyly Carte career playing Bill Bobstay, he was now asked to play Dick Deadeye instead. And this – not bad for someone who had been in the Company less than two months – was without question promotion; for Dick Deadeye, unlike Bobstay, was seen as a principal part throughout the D'Oyly Carte years. Insofar as acting and singing can be separated in G&S, it is above all an acting part. Not only does Deadeye have no song of his own. He has little solo singing altogether.

So Deadeye became Billington's second *Pinafore* part; and Deadeye continued to be his part when in mid-December he was transferred to another of Carte's companies then about to open for a week in Exeter, a week immediately followed by a fortnight in Torquay. And it was while this Company were in Torquay that he was given an opportunity to play a third G&S role.

The date was Tuesday December 30th. That afternoon the Company assembled in the adjacent town of Paignton to give a single performance of the opera that was to follow *HMS Pinafore* in the G&S sequence: *The Pirates of Penzance*. Gilbert and Sullivan themselves were then in America, about to present the first proper performance of *Pirates* in New York. The Paignton performance was put on simply to secure the opera's copyright in Britain.

The arrangements for this performance were undertaken by Helen Lenoir, who had come down to Torquay in person primarily for that purpose. It was a performance given after just one rehearsal. It was a performance for which the performers made no attempt to learn their lines or their music – they did not, anyway, have the full score. It was a performance which they played throughout in the costumes they wore for *Pinafore*.

And there among them was Fred Billington, dressed as Dick Deadeye but cast as the "highly nervous" Sergeant of Police who makes such an impact in the new opera's second act. But inappropriate costume though it was, inadequate in every way though the performance might be, the occasion was another significant landmark in his career.

The Sergeant of Police was the only part in G&S that he was in any sense to create. But it was one of the parts that, in the years to come, he would most clearly make his own.

ROYAL BIJOU THEATRE,

PAIGNTON.

FOR ONE DAY ONLY,
TUESDAY, DECEMBER 30TH,

AT TWO O'CLOCK.

AN ENTIRELY NEW AND ORIGINAL

✶ OPERA ✶

By Messrs. W. S. GILBERT and ARTHUR SULLIVAN, entitled

THE PIRATES OF PENZANCE,
OR LOVE AND DUTY,

Being its first production in any country.

MAJOR-GENERAL	MR. RICHARD MANSFIELD
THE PIRATE KING	MR. FEDERICI
FREDERICK (a Pirate)	MR. CADWALADR
SAMUEL ⎫ JAMES ⎭ Pirates	⎰ MR. LACKNER ⎱ MR. LEHAY
SERGEANT OF POLICE	MR. BILLINGTON
MABEL	MISS PETRELLI
EDITH	MISS MAY
ISABEL	MISS K. NEVILLE
KATE	MISS MONMOUTH
RUTH (Frederick's Nurse)	MISS FANNY HARRISON

SCENE

ACT I.	A CAVERN BY THE SEA SHORE.
ACT II.	A RUINED CHAPEL BY MOONLIGHT.

Doors open at 1.30. Commence at 2.

Sofa Stalls, 3/-; Second Seats, 2/-; Area, 1/-; Gallery, 6d.

TICKETS TO BE HAD AT THE GERSTON HOTEL.

Conductor, Mr. RALPH HORNER.   Acting Manager, Mr. HERBERT BROOK.

Rutland Barrington and the Pooh-Bah Parts

"My own idea is that Pooh-Bah is the greatest man in the operas. He is a great character even if he is so utterly impossible … We all know the men whose life ambition it is to have a finger in every pie in the making."

(A.H. Godwin, Gilbert & Sullivan, 1926)

So having duly, in however sketchy a manner, played the Sergeant of Police, Fred Billington now had three G&S roles under his not inconsiderable belt. In all, as I mentioned in the Introduction, he was to play eighteen such roles, and of those roles no fewer than eleven were associated with the name of Rutland Barrington. As far as Barrington was concerned, those roles fell into two categories: the ones he created, and the ones he didn't create but would play on some occasion later. Accordingly it's now time to consider the origin and development of those roles as they related to Barrington, and why in consequence certain aspects of those roles are as they are.

So, first, here is a list of the roles he (Barrington) played. The four asterisked are the ones he didn't create, but played instead in this or that eventual revival:

Trial by Jury:	Counsel*; Judge*
The Sorcerer:	Dr Daly
HMS Pinafore:	Captain Corcoran

The Pirates of Penzance:	Sergeant of Police
Patience:	Archibald Grosvenor
Iolanthe:	Lord Mountararat
Princess Ida:	King Hildebrand
The Mikado:	Pooh-Bah
Ruddigore:	Sir Despard Murgatroyd
The Yeomen of the Guard:	Wilfred Shadbolt*
The Gondoliers:	Giuseppe; Don Alhambra*
Utopia Limited:	King Paramount
The Grand Duke:	Ludwig

With the exception of the Counsel, the Judge, Mountararat and Giuseppe, these parts have always been known collectively as the "Barrington parts". With the exception of these four parts again, but with the eventual addition of Private Willis in *Iolanthe*, they are also sometimes known as the "heavy comedian parts".

There is no question that Barrington's contribution to the success and popularity of G&S in the operas' early days was enormous and long lasting in its effects. He put his mark on them right from his first appearance when he was engaged to play Dr Daly in the original production of *The Sorcerer*; and it's not even too fanciful to suggest that the impact he made in that production outdid the impact made by every other member of the cast. Here from the *Era* is the most substantial – and most gushing – of the many plaudits he received for his performance:

"In Mr Barrington's delineation of Dr Daly, the sentimental vicar, we have one of the most original creations of the modern stage. Nature has favoured Mr Barrington with a handsome face and a stately figure, and when he steps upon the stage as the Vicar of Ploverleigh the illusion is absolutely perfect. All the artificial aids of the stage are forgotten at once. The mild, meek, gentle representative of the church in a country village appears 'in his habit as he lived'. Surely this is not an actor, not a person who has studied a part line by line, who has committed to memory particulars of exits and entrances, who has meditated upon the mysteries of stage 'business'. No, a thousand times no …

Seriously the lifelike manner in which Mr Barrington depicts some of the harmless peculiarities and mannerisms of a country vicar is positively remarkable. One would suppose he had spent every Sunday of his life in the pulpit, and that his daily life was devoted to the work of a remote parish … The attitudes, the tones, the vocalisation, even the most trifling details, are carefully studied. The actor is never 'out of the character' for a moment.

Take it for all in all, it is one of the most delightful impersonations we have ever witnessed …"

And the plaudits he received for his performances in all the operas that followed, if not quite as fulsome as this, were mostly – not always, but mostly – highly complimentary.

He gained such plaudits, moreover, despite a widely acknowledged downside. That downside had nothing to do with his acting but rather with his singing voice, which was of variable quality at best. There is the well-known story of somebody once commenting to Gilbert that at a certain performance Barrington had actually sung in tune, prompting the response: "Don't worry, it won't last". And Sullivan, in writing the music for his parts, always kept his vocal limitations and deficiencies in mind, even if Barrington himself didn't always appreciate the fact.

"It is scarcely necessary to remind Mr Barrington that Sir Arthur Sullivan was often a good deal more than a lifeboat to him," once said the longstanding D'Oyly Carte Musical Director Francois Cellier – this after Barrington had publicly suggested that the orchestra in a theatre should be a "lifebuoy of support" to the singer and not a gigantic wave to drown him. "Indeed in one particular phrase in *Patience* Sir Arthur put in a strenuous note for the sole purpose of saving Mr Barrington from falling overboard."

Similarly, and even more emphatically, Gilbert devised parts aimed at maximising Barrington's acting strengths, just as he did the acting strengths of every other member of the Opera Comique, and later Savoy, Theatre Company. Those strengths in Barrington's case were, first, a jovial, larger-than-life stage personality underpinned by an unshakable self-confidence or, not to mince words, an unshakable conceit; and, second, what may best be described as an unflappable stolidity. In addition he seems to have been another of those people who, even in their youth, have something middle-aged about them. He was indeed only twenty-four when he first played the elderly Dr Daly, which made his performance in the part still more remarkable.

Then there was his build. Though reasonably slim at the outset of his G&S career, it wasn't long before he started putting on weight. The line "I am much taller and much stouter than I was", for instance, that Gilbert gave him in *Patience* was not put in by accident.

Similarly Ko-Ko's description of Pooh-Bah (i.e. Barrington) in *The Mikado* – "That is a Tremendous Swell" – can surely be taken to refer as much to his size as to his grandiose public standing. And by the time of *The Gondoliers* and he was launched as Giuseppe he was unquestionably overweight – no less than "very fat", as the not exactly sylph-like Queen Victoria described him in her Journal when he played the part in a "command" performance of the Venetian opera in Windsor Castle. Enough said.

Because of all this Barrington was hardly cut out to play the young romantic lover. It has always surprised me he was chosen for Giuseppe, given that the latter and his fellow-gondolier Marco come the closest to being genuinely romantic young lovers in the whole of Gilbert and Sullivan. For Marco G&S went for a performer – Courtice Pounds – who had the required romantic qualities in spades. Did they really want their Giuseppe, with whom Marco acts in tandem throughout the opera, to be any less romantic, never mind being fat

Rutland Barrington
(Author's collection)

as well? Wouldn't the proper part for Barrington in *The Gondoliers* have been the Grand Inquisitor, Don Alhambra?

The answer to that question is of course "yes". But though he was to play "The Don" eventually, it was his own fault that he missed out doing so first time round. Throughout the run of the previous opera, *The Yeomen of the Guard*, he had been away from G&S initially trying his hand at theatrical management. Because of this, the part he would surely have had in *Yeomen* had he been around, Wilfred Shadbolt, had gone instead to a D'Oyly Carte newcomer, W.H. Denny.

Denny was accordingly the man in possession when the writing of *The Gondoliers* was getting under way. As Shadbolt he had fitted into the G&S scheme of things without, apparently, any problem. And because of this Gilbert, Sullivan and Carte had seen no need either to demote or dump him even though Barrington, his management venture having previously fizzled out, was now available again.

Barrington played Giuseppe almost as though he'd decided the part was a comic lead rather than that of a young man in love; and he initially enraged Gilbert by indulging in more than a little "gagging". But while he was surely miscast as a romantic lover, he could certainly play the comic lover, as he had proved first as Dr Daly, later as Grosvenor, and in due course as Sir Despard in *Ruddigore*.

Even so there were three of his parts in which he was not required to play the lover, comic or otherwise, in any real sense at all: the Sergeant of Police, King Hildebrand and, most importantly, Pooh-Bah; while even Mountararat could loosely be said to come into the same bracket. And one consequence of all this was that whereas, for example, the G&S *tenor* plays mostly opposite the soprano, the only female performer who can be substantially linked in the same way with any of the Barrington characters is the soubrette.

The soubrette who played opposite Barrington himself in those characters was – it need hardly be said – Jessie Bond. Jessie Bond first played opposite him as Constance to his Dr Daly in the first London revival of *The Sorcerer*. Later she played Pitti-Sing to his (unromantic) Pooh-Bah, Mad Margaret to his Sir Despard and Tessa to his Giuseppe, and she would have been Phoebe to his Wilfred Shadbolt had he been in the original production of *The Yeomen of the Guard*.

No less than Barrington, Jessie Bond had a compelling stage personality. Surprisingly in a way, for her sense of self-importance matched his own, they gelled together well both on stage and off it – so much so that in 1891 Barrington devised a programme for the two of them of "musical duologues and monologues" which they then toured together for several weeks.

But in terms of Barrington's career in D'Oyly Carte, the performer who most obviously defined his position in G&S was not Jessie Bond or any other soubrette. Rather it was one of the Company's other male performers. That other male performer was George Grossmith.

Like Barrington, George Grossmith made his D'Oyly Carte debut in the original production of *The Sorcerer*. The role Gilbert and Sullivan handed to

Grossmith was that of the sorcerer himself, John Wellington Wells; and what linked him and Barrington so closely was the fact that they were the two members of the Company who played the chief "comedian" roles. If Dr Daly was the "heavy" comedian's part in the opera, John Wellington Wells was the part for the "light" comedian; and from the word go Grossmith played that part as though he'd been preparing to play it from birth.

Because, however, the plotting and writing of *The Sorcerer* had been more or less completed before they chose him for the opera, Gilbert and Sullivan made no attempt to ensure that he and Barrington had a scene in it together – the paths of Wells and Dr Daly scarcely cross on stage at all. But the fact that they both slotted into their *Sorcerer* parts so well clearly alerted G&S to the possibilities inherent in having them play opposite each other when future operas came to be written.

Those possibilities were duly exploited, first, in *HMS Pinafore,* with Barrington playing Captain Corcoran and Grossmith Sir Joseph Porter; then in *Patience* when the two of them were cast as the rival poets, Grosvenor and Bunthorne; in *Princess Ida* when they became the rival kings, Hildebrand and Gama; in *The Mikado* when they played, respectively, Pooh-Bah and Ko-Ko; in *Ruddigore* when they played Sir Despard and Robin Oakapple; while in *Yeomen* Barrington, had he been available, would have played Wilfred Shadbolt to Grossmith's Jack Point.

As a pair of comedians they made the classic contrast: Barrington the taller – much the taller – stolid and solid, economic in movement, avuncular, suave, unctuous; Grossmith short, dapper, mercurial, light on his feet and, even when apparently relaxed, busy and chock-full of energy.

Theoretically in the Company they were on an equal footing. And not only on an equal footing with each other but, at least at the beginning, with the rest of the principals as well, since Gilbert and Sullivan were determined their Company should have no stars. But this was one area – one of the few areas – in which G&S failed to convert theory into practice. For there's no doubt that both Grossmith and Barrington were seen by the London public as stars, whatever their mentors might like to think.

Yet were the two of them seen, performance-wise, as equal with each other? Without taking anything away from Grossmith's success as John Wellington Wells, Barrington, as I've already implied, probably had the edge over him with regard to *The Sorcerer*. This was on the one hand because Dr Daly has considerably more to do than Wells, and on the other because audiences relished a Gilbertian vicar even more than they relished a Gilbertian sorcerer. As an *Era* reporter was noting after *The Sorcerer* had been on the boards no more than three weeks, several "well-known clergymen" had already gone to the opera specifically to "have a quiet chuckle at their reverend brother on the stage". And in Victorian times, with the widespread belief among the "respectable" classes that the theatre was a place of immorality and sin, this was quite something.

But thereafter, with one or possibly two exceptions (see below) it was a different story. Thereafter there was no question in most people's minds that the Company's top star was Grossmith. It was the irresistible comic attraction of the "little man" that did it; and in effect G&S sanctioned this development themselves, by making Grossmith's parts central to the action and plot of each of the operas in turn, by the patter songs and sheer quantity of solo numbers they gave him to sing, and by the brief but inspired bursts of comic dancing they offered him the chance to incorporate into his various portrayals. Nothing – or, at least, very little – they gave Barrington ultimately equalled the package of advantages they gave "G.G".

The way things were to go was duly shown straight away with their respective parts in *Pinafore*. Sir Joseph Porter, Grossmith's *Pinafore* part, is an irrepressible stage character in a way that Captain Corcoran, Barrington's part, never quite has the opportunity to match, good though the part is in itself. Similarly in *Princess Ida*, Grossmith's part of King Gama is a much more effective stage character than Barrington's part of King Hildebrand.

Or consider Ko-Ko and Pooh-Bah in *The Mikado*. Pooh-Bah (Barrington's part) is a splendid part for any performer. But – and it's a significant but – Pooh-Bah has just one solo number to Ko-Ko's two and – an equally significant and curious fact – it's perfectly possible to relate the basic story of *The Mikado* without mentioning Pooh-Bah even once.

Most significant of all, though, when assessing their respective contributions to G&S, were the parts allotted to the two of them in *Iolanthe*. Grossmith was cast as the Lord Chancellor, a figure who would stand out on any comic stage. By comparison Barrington's part, Lord Mountararat, though another good part in itself, stands much less chance of making the same impact, if only because he is throughout one of a pair with the tenor, Lord Tolloller. There seem not to have been many people at the time of *Iolanthe's* opening who spotted this, but one person who did was the critic from the London *Entr'acte*. In previous operas, suggested this critic,

> "Mr Grossmith and Mr Barrington have been favoured with parts of about equal strength, but in *Iolanthe* an evident new departure has been made, and Mr Barrington has to content himself by playing a palpable second fiddle."

And even though (the writer added) he played it "very well too", that didn't alter the overall imbalance.

The one undoubted exception to all this was *The Pirates of Penzance* in which Barrington, as the Sergeant of Police, came quickly to be seen as having the edge over the Major-General, which was the part given to Grossmith. If Barrington himself is to be believed, G&S created the Sergeant's part without initially considering him for it at all – or so he wrote in his autobiography. But having eventually secured it he added, with what can only be called his usual cheerful conceit:

> "It turned out one of my greatest successes. It is an abnormally short part, being only on view seventeen minutes in all. I timed it one night, but into those seventeen minutes were crowded countless opportunities

of 'scoring', of all of which, I am proud to remember, Gilbert told me I took full advantage."

The other opera in which there's a possible case for suggesting that Barrington had a better deal than Grossmith was *Ruddigore*. While Sir Despard (Barrington's part) is much the shorter part, it has a sustained comic intensity that Grossmith's part of Robin Oakapple never quite equals, perhaps for the very reason that the character, as one first night critic put it, is "seldom off the stage". "Over-exposure" might be another way of describing it; and, interestingly, Barrington was to suffer this sort of over-exposure himself in the parts he was given in the last two G&S operas, *Utopia Limited* and *The Grand Duke.*

But to emphasise the main point again. Great though Barrington's successes as the Sergeant of Police and Sir Despard undoubtedly were, this didn't alter the fact that, overall, G&S dealt Grossmith the stronger hand and did so quite deliberately. The result was that, throughout the D'Oyly Carte span, the player of the Grossmith parts almost always had the greater share of the limelight, the greater share of the applause, was given the greater number of encores, and was almost always seen as being the Company's biggest name and, when necessary, its spokesman. Only two of the performers who played the Pooh-Bah parts down the years achieved anything like a similar status. One of these, as will be seen in later chapters of this book, was Fred Billington. The other, right at the end of the span, was Kenneth Sandford. And both owed their elevation to that status at least partly to long service.

So did this mean the Barrington/Pooh-Bah performers almost always came off second best in any D'Oyly Carte popularity contest, or in terms of what today might be called job satisfaction? In one sense – the sense we've been talking about – the answer was clearly "yes".

But in another sense it was "not necessarily". If the Grossmith/light comedian performer was a performer who totally relished the limelight and wallowed in the attention bestowed on him, that was fine. And if, as part of this, he could never get enough applause, never get enough praise, never get enough opportunities to be the centre of attention, that was finer still. As someone of whom all that could be said, the person who immediately springs to mind is Henry Lytton, the G&S light comedian supreme.

That was one way of looking at the situation. Yet there was another way – and from the Pooh-Bah player's viewpoint a more positive way - of looking at it; which could be expressed like this:

Until the late 1960s the light comedian almost always had a part in all the full-length operas. That meant he was "on" at every performance – or, at least, his audiences *expected* him to be on at every performance. Not only that, but they expected him, as the star, to be on top form at every performance – which meant seven or eight performances a week – and to be outgoing, ready to sign autographs and chat to all-comers at the stage door after every performance. And all this he could find immensely burdensome, especially if he was by nature highly strung and unrelaxed. The person who most obviously comes to mind here is Peter Pratt, the Ko-Ko *et al* of the 1950s, a diffident perfectionist on whom the strains and demands of the job eventually took a definite toll.

And this was where the Pooh-Bah player in the Company came to have the better deal. For the greater part of the Company's existence the Pooh-Bah player, whoever he was, rarely found himself being asked to play in all the operas being performed at any one time, which thereby gave him occasional - and sometimes even more than occasional - nights "off". This policy, as will be seen, would actually be initiated with Fred Billington in 1905.

Having one or more operas off immediately reduced the strain on the performer, whether this was Billington himself or any of his several successors. Unless that performer saw himself as the Company's top attraction, the man audiences came to see ahead of everyone else (and it's probably fair to say that, of all the Pooh-Bah players, only Rutland Barrington viewed himself in this light), he had all the advantages of a high profile without the strain and extra responsibility that goes with being the top person in any sphere of life.

All that, I freely admit, is only a personal opinion based on the way I think about these things myself. But it's always seemed to me that, provided he was able to accept being the lesser in status of the two D'Oyly Carte comedians, the Pooh-Bah player had the best of both worlds.

Rutland Barrington as the Sergeant of Police
(Collection: Tony Gower)

On Tour, 1880-84

"Once on tour we had a military chorister with us, and during a crossing we made from Belfast to Liverpool, the Isle of Man hove in sight. I was walking the deck when the chorister asked 'What place is that, sir?' When I answered 'China' he looked a bit surprised and said 'Gorblimey, don't we get abart!' "

(Fred Billington)

The Paignton performance of *The Pirates of Penzance* at the end of December 1879 was for some time a "one off" in every sense. It wasn't till the following April that the new opera had its first performance in London. And it wasn't till October that it began its first run in the provinces – and then by a different Company from the one that had played it in Paignton.

For Fred Billington the new year, 1880 – his first full year in D'Oyly Carte – didn't feature *Pirates* at all. Rather it continued for him with *HMS Pinafore*, in which he played throughout the year and, from March onwards, *The Sorcerer*, in which of course he was playing for the first time. In *Pinafore* that year he played both his previous parts, Bobstay and Deadeye; while in *The Sorcerer* he also played two parts, first the small part of the Notary, then graduating to the much more substantial part of Dr Daly.

The following year, 1881, it was Deadeye and Dr Daly again. How did his performances in those two parts come across? The *Bath Chronicle* that May offered a somewhat mixed verdict:

"Mr Fred Billington sang, but scarcely looked or acted, the triangular Dick Deadeye. We much prefer his Dr Daly of the previous evening"

while two weeks later his performance in the latter part elicited a not entirely favourable comment from the *Bristol Times and Mirror*:

"Mr Billington [is] a capital Dr Daly, if a bit too stiff."

But in other places it was a much less ambivalent story. When that same May he returned for the first time as a professional performer to his home town in Yorkshire, the local *Chronicle* had no such reservations:

"[Dr Daly and Dick Deadeye were played by] Mr Fred Billington, a native of Huddersfield, whose good stage presence, quiet, self-contained acting and substantial baritone voice gained for him well-deserved plaudits"

and similarly the previous year when, once again playing his original *Pinafore* part, he paid his first visit to another Yorkshire town, it was clear he produced exactly the performance required of him there:

"The ship has a good Boatswain on board in the person of Mr F. Billington, who excited the usual amount of enthusiasm in 'He is an Englishman'."

(*Sheffield Daily Telegraph*)

Furthermore, whatever criticism he may occasionally have received, it didn't stop the D'Oyly Carte management giving him new parts when the opportunity arose to do so. That November he played for the first time in a proper production of *The Pirates of Penzance* – and not, as might be expected, as the Sergeant of Police but as the Pirate King, a far more substantial part which he continued to play throughout the next year, 1882, as well. And 1882 also saw him in a new *Pinafore* part, that of Captain Corcoran:

"Mr F. Billington makes a capital Captain Corcoran, the true nautical gait with which he walks the quarter-deck showing that he has studied his role to advantage."

(*Western Morning News*, Plymouth)

They noticed things like a nautical gait in Plymouth.

Then to Corcoran and the Pirate King was added, in 1883, Private Willis in the previous year's new opera, *Iolanthe*. Here's the *Bath Chronicle* again:

Billington as Dr Daly, c.1898
(Collection: Tony Gower)

"We were pleased to hear Private Willis of the Grenadier Guards sing in tune, and must compliment Mr F. Billington upon his work."

It was the second time in ten months that a D'Oyly Carte Company had brought *Iolanthe* to Bath. Presumably George Marler, the Private Willis first time round, had *not* sung in tune.

Then in 1884, following *Iolanthe*, came *Princess Ida*, in which Billington was cast as King Hildebrand:

"Mr Fred Billington is a manly King Hildebrand, and sings as well as he acts."

(*Bristol Times and Mirror*)

"Mr Fred Billington was highly successful as King Hildebrand, and not only sang well but delivered his lines with great clearness."
(*Era* correspondent, Brighton)

So by mid-1884, by which time he was aged thirty and had been with D'Oyly Carte five years, Billington had played nine G&S parts. Surprisingly, given how he later came to be defined by the "Barrington" parts, only four of those parts – Dr Daly, Captain Corcoran, the Sergeant of Police and King Hildebrand – were parts which Barrington had played himself. Most significant of the other parts – that is, in terms of their original performer – were Dick Deadeye and the Pirate King, bass parts which had been created in London by Richard Temple, who later went on to create, most notably, the title-role in *The Mikado*.

But as well as his G&S parts during his early D'Oyly Carte years, Billington also played in a couple of non-G&S short pieces. Adding short pieces to the main item on the programme was a fairly common practice in Victorian musical theatre, and during the first two decades of the D'Oyly Carte span the various Carte companies followed this practice extensively, performing a stream of short works as curtain-raisers and afterpieces to go with most of the G&S operas which were their stable performing fare. *The Love Test*, mentioned in the announcement on page 14, was one such. And there's no need to even think of repeating the fact that *Trial by Jury* was another.

The first of such pieces in which Billington appeared was a "comedietta" called *Antony and Cleopatra*. This piece, possibly a play without music, had been added to the programme for a time during his first *Pinafore* tour in 1879, and in it he had played a character called Policeman 100A. So despite its title, it obviously wasn't Shakespeare.

The second piece, however, was a musical piece without any question, being described as "a new and original operetta", and was called *Six-and-Six*. An *Era* correspondent gave it a brief review when it was performed in

Liverpool in August and September 1880 and, as he made clear, it wasn't so much an operetta as a musical farce:

> "The scene of the little musical work is laid in a matrimonial registry [that is, agency] office, kept by a lively and interesting gentleman named Mr Sysiphus Twister. Here there are a succession of ludicrous situations consequent upon the rapid arrival of clients on matrimony bent, and the difficulty which the chief of the establishment has in keeping their presence unknown to each other. After a good many laughable incidents, the various applicants are mated, and the curtain descends on a chorus of general jubilation. The libretto is sparkling and catching, and there are some parts of [the] music which are worth remembering."

Sysiphus Twister himself was played by Billington, and it doesn't take a genius to work out what kind of person *he* was supposed to be. During its run *Six-and-Six* was played in tandem with *HMS Pinafore* and *The Sorcerer*.

Nor were these two short pieces the only non-G&S works in which Billington appeared during these years, for there was a period of seven to eight months beginning at Christmas 1882 which he spent as a G&S exile touring in a production of an opera called *Rip Van Winkle*.

From the *Era*, April 21st 1883:

> "Theatre Royal, Nottingham. Planquette's opera *Rip Van Winkle*, since re-christened *Rip*, was produced here on Monday last with every sign of success and, we may add, deservedly so.
>
> The subject is interesting, the music charming – although, perhaps, not quite so original in some places as might be looked for – the artists fully up to their work, the dresses quaint and characteristic [that is, in character] and the scenery and stage appointments the perfection of good taste."

"The perfection of good taste" makes it sound like a D'Oyly Carte production, and a D'Oyly Carte production indeed it was, played by yet another D'Oyly Carte touring Company. In *Rip* Billington played not one part but two – characters named Derrick von Slous and Captain Hendrich Hudson – though he was not the only member of the cast to whom this applied. Esme Lee, the principal soprano and another temporary exile from G&S, found herself playing two characters likewise.

Given most of the above, it might appear that Billington's early career was largely spent in just one D'Oyly Carte Company, but that was some way from being the case. Throughout the 1880s Richard D'Oyly Carte had a number of G&S companies touring simultaneously, in consequence of which any performer on the Company's books was potentially liable at any time to be switched from one Company to another according to operational needs.

Moreover the companies themselves could not be considered entirely stable units, for there was a continuing process by which they were formed, disbanded and then, as often as not, re-formed under a different designation or name. For the record here is a chronological list of the companies in which Fred Billington played during the first five years of the 1880s, and showing which of his parts he took in each case:

1880:	Second *Pinafore* Company:	Deadeye
	"D" Company:	Notary; Bobstay; Dr Daly; Deadeye
	"A" Company:	Deadeye
1881:	"B" Company:	Dr Daly; Deadeye; Pirate King
1882:	"B" Company:	Corcoran; Pirate King
1883:	"*Pinafore* and *Pirates*" Company:	Corcoran; Pirate King
	Number 2 *Iolanthe* Company:	Private Willis
1884:	"D" (*Princess Ida* Number 1) Company:	Hildebrand
	"A" (*Princess Ida* Number 2) Company:	Hildebrand

Touring.

Whereas Rutland Barrington's entire D'Oyly Carte career was spent in London, Billington was to spend all but a small portion of his career on tour. The second half of the nineteenth century and the first half of the twentieth century – a period that encompassed Billington's lifetime and more – was the period that saw British theatrical touring reach its heyday. The majority of actors in those years reckoned to spend a large part of their working lives "on the road", as it was called, and the *Era* each week published a list showing which companies would be performing in which towns during the week ahead.

It was the coming of the railways and the rapidly expanding rail network that had enabled this to happen. A journalist writing in the periodical the *Theatre* in October 1880 went all pseudo-poetic about what the existence of the railways could mean to the theatre *critic* of the time:

"Many thanks to you who invented railway engines, and to your worthy followers, for in your grand iron steeds you have furnished me with most excellent substitutes for those attributes of the immortal – wings! And by your aid I have travelled many miles during the past few weeks to see the theatrical novelties of that region called 'the provinces'."

Thanks likewise to the railways, theatre companies could get to most towns, large or small, anywhere in the country. During his years in D'Oyly Carte Fred Billington played at least once in the staggering total of between one hundred and seventy and one hundred and eighty towns in England, Wales, Scotland and Ireland, as well as more than twenty "local" theatres in London. The touring life, naturally enough, didn't suit everyone. But, as he quickly found, it certainly suited *him*.

It was to some extent a case of getting used to its routine. That routine consisted for the most part of performing in a particular town from Monday to Saturday, then moving on to the next town on the Sunday, or from time to time the Sunday after that. ("Actors and fish travel on Sundays" as a contemporary aphorism had it). The "next town", moreover, wasn't necessarily just round the next bend but might be umpteen miles away. To take just two random examples involving Billington in his first year of touring, 1880. On June 13th he and "D" Company travelled from Leicester right up to Edinburgh; on August 22nd they went from Buxton in Derbyshire to Douglas on the Isle of Man.

Details of any of these journeys, though, are hard to find. Very little was written about life in the Carte companies on these early tours, whether by Billington or anyone else. This was partly due to the fact that few performers are natural writers or feel at ease putting pen to paper. But it was no less a consequence of their being almost constantly on the move, quite apart from having to give six or seven performances every week of the touring year.

And added to all this there was the need, in each town they played, to find and arrange digs. Even though there was no shortage of theatrical digs in those days, finding suitable ones – or ones that were at least tolerable – took up a considerable slice of every performer's time. So what, if anything, can be said about Billington and digs?

The answer – surprisingly, given how little can be said about him in connection with travelling – is "a fair amount". And it's in connection with digs – or, more accurately in his case, accommodation – that the picture of him as a touring actor most clearly emerges.

For although he may well have *begun* his touring days in digs, it was not long before he decided that digs as such, with all the inadequacies and discomforts that so often went with them, were not for him, and he only went for this type of accommodation on rare occasions thereafter. Instead, week in week out, he ensconced himself in hotels – one hotel after another – or if not in hotels, then in guest houses – and went on doing this for virtually the next four decades. He became the archetypal theatrical vagabond; a man of – literally – no fixed abode.

Hotels four decades on were probably much the same as they'd been in the 1880s, or at any rate had not changed radically. George Grossmith, after leaving D'Oyly Carte in 1889, spent many years touring the country as a solo entertainer. During these years he stayed in any number of hotels himself, and in his second volume of reminiscences, *Piano and I*, published in 1910, he made reference to some of these – references not all of which were favourable:

"One hotel I went to – a small inn – there was apparently no one in charge of it at all. My secretary rang the bell, and after some delay a seedy-looking 'boots' appeared. His mouth was crammed full, and I could not quite hear what he said. My secretary said: 'Is there nobody here to attend to us, to take off the luggage, etc?'
He replied: 'Orlrionemolomeslur!'
I presume he meant: 'All right – one moment, sir'."

The name and location of this hotel Grossmith was careful not to mention; and which hotels in which places Fred Billington stayed in during the course of his D'Oyly Carte travels is something that can be ascertained with certainty in only a few instances. Hotels, even if they are still in business, are hardly likely

The Royal Hotel, Bury. Not, unfortunately, the building in which Billington was staying when the 1901 census was taken, but a former hotel on the same site demolished in the 1890s in which he may well have stayed previously
(Collection: Bury Museum)

to have kept records of who stayed in them going back a century and more; and I have been able to pinpoint just six, as follows:

The Queen's Hotel, Folkestone
The Saracen's Head Hotel, Hanley
The Castle Inn, Preston
The Royal Hotel, Bury
The Gresham Hotel, Dublin
The Great Eastern Hotel, London

Of these, the Queen's Hotel in Folkestone and the Saracen's Head Hotel in Hanley get on the list because they were hotels at which Billington received letters – letters, that is, that have survived; while the Castle Inn in Preston and the Royal Hotel in Bury were hotels in which he happened to be staying on the days when census counts were taken in 1881 and 1901 respectively.

The Castle Inn, standing in Preston's Market Place, was listed in a contemporary Preston directory as the Castle and Commercial Hotel. At the time of the 1881 census its proprietor was a lady – "Mary Rich (widow)" as she was rather winsomely described – rich widows can't have been all that common among Victorian hotel keepers. In that census Billington was recorded as a "visitor" in the hotel and an actor, though he was also put down as having been born in Manchester – not a city that a Yorkshireman would have specially relished being described as his birthplace.

That at least was rectified in the census taken in 1901 when his birthplace was correctly given as Lockwood. This time he was described as a "comedian" rather than an actor, while again being recorded as a hotel "visitor". The Royal Hotel in Silver Street in central Bury, the hotel in question, was one of the town's leading commercial hotels; and, as an interesting detail, the census also revealed that, as well as the landlord and his wife and daughter, the place had a staff of no fewer than eleven servants, including two waiters, two barmaids, a cook, a laundress and a nurse – providing, it might be thought, just about everything a visiting comedian could possibly want.

The fifth hotel which can be identified as one in which Billington stayed – and stayed on several occasions – is the Gresham Hotel in Dublin. His name would most likely have shown up there on the 1891 census, given that he was in a Company playing Dublin's Gaiety Theatre on the relevant date, but for the fact that these records were among a plethora of documents later destroyed in a fire. In addition, a letter of his survives that was actually written on the hotel's own notepaper (see page 39) and that dated from the time the Company played another of their Dublin seasons in June 1905.

The Gresham Hotel had been founded in 1817 by Thomas Gresham, previously a butler in the house of a prominent local family. How he acquired the capital to found a hotel is not known. But found it he did, and it flourished. It flourished in Billington's time and it flourishes still. It has been described as "Ireland's most famous hotel", and it will be mentioned again later in this book.

The sixth hotel on the list – the Great Eastern Hotel in London – will also be mentioned again in due course. Suffice to say for the moment that it opened in 1884; that it adjoins Liverpool Street Station, one of the major London termini; that it was a prominent example of the many hotels built all over the country to cater for the needs of the ever-increasing railway travelling public; and that it was another hotel in which Billington stayed on several occasions.

So there he (Billington) was moving time after time from one hotel to the next, turning up with his luggage one Sunday, then paying his bill and leaving, still with luggage in tow, one or two Sundays later. How did he spend his spare time – the mornings, afternoons, and late evenings after performances – in these establishments?

The first thing to say is that he was invariably a familiar presence in the hotel dining room. He was a man who, more than anything, loved his food – any food, though he was particularly fond of meat. Having come through his initial period of "hard up" times, he was able to indulge himself, where food was concerned, as much as he wanted, and his reputation as a big eater was widespread.

It even found an echo in his performances in G&S. "The humour of his delivery of Pooh-Bah's line in *The Mikado*, 'I don't want any lunch', was immense," wrote a journalist acquaintance on his death, "and for his friends it had additional point as poor Fred always wanted his lunch. He was a great trencherman."

Indeed the words "lunch" or "dinner" or food in general had only to be mentioned by anyone in his hearing to pretty well ensure he'd be there, wherever it was, ready to indulge. Thus he was to be found one evening in 1884 at the end-of-season supper organised by the *Princess Ida* Number 1 Company's Cricket Club, even though – for all he was a Yorkshireman – he took no part in any D'Oyly Carte cricket matches himself.

In consequence of all this, though, it was not long before he started putting on weight. That said, however, it must immediately be stressed that nobody, least of all himself, thought badly of him for allowing this to happen. Putting on weight in those days was regarded as a sign of prosperity, an indication that a man was successful in life – which is not to say that in Billington's case it didn't evoke an occasional comment that was less than flattering.

One such comment became the punchline of an anecdote related by Lindsay Harman, a D'Oyly Carte chorister and small part player of the 1890s, which makes the point unashamedly. We're back to Dublin, the Gaiety Theatre and the Gresham Hotel once more.

It was late one evening. The performance at the theatre was not long over. The heavy, well-padded Billington emerged into the street outside where he called a cab, and

"was just about to enter it when the Stage Manager, Mr J. Scanlan, invited him into his, saying he was passing Billington's hotel and would drop him on his way.

36

The offer was accepted, so Billy tipped his own cabby a shilling, saying he would not require him. The cabby scratched his head, and hoped His Honour would give him more than a shilling.

'What, you scamp, when I never got into your cab?' said Billy.

'But consider the fright Your Honour put us into – me and the old horse,' replied Pat"

and there is no questioning the assumption that this remark alluded to Billington's bulk.

Second only to food among his life's pleasures was chat – sitting and talking. Billington was a great one for sitting and talking, and keeping other people chained to their seats, even if they needed to get away, while he was yacking on. "One always missed trains when talking to Fred Billington," as one of his friends laughingly put it. And as most of the hotels in which he stayed would have had at least one public room in which residents and their friends could meet, he had ample opportunities to sit and chat as much as he wanted. The public room was as likely as not labelled the "Smoking Room". The Smoking Room was intrinsically a male preserve. And what a room of that description in a somewhat downmarket hotel of the time was like was trenchantly described by George Grossmith. The atmosphere might be rumbustiously cheerful, but the chairs were likely to be uncomfortable, and

"I was nearly suffocated by the smoke. Cheap pipes, cheap tobacco, cheap cigars and still cheaper cigarettes (halfpenny a packet of ten)"

and that was a description penned by a man who, like most men of the time, was a confirmed smoker himself.

None of this, though, would have bothered Billington who would liberally contribute to the fug on his own account. He smoked, according to one source, "very heavy, dark, shaggy tobacco". According to another source, he went in for fourteen-inch cigars. And somehow all that food, all that sitting around, all that chatting and smoking fitted together. More surprisingly for someone who unquestionably liked company, he also had times when he made it clear he wanted to be on his own. According to a third source he was a great reader – which meant more sitting around still.

All that sitting around, whether in company or on his own, came without any exercise to balance it, except on stage. In later years he would play golf and get exercise that way. But he was not to be found on the golf course very often, if ever, during his early D'Oyly Carte days. Nor, as already indicated, was he to be found in any of the cricket teams formed by the various Carte companies on tour.

But mention of Billington in connection with those cricket teams throws up an unexpected query. For one of the people whose name does feature in those teams for the three years 1882-84 was a certain W.O. Billington. So who was W.O. Billington? Was he Fred's younger brother Walter?

The answer is almost certainly "no" – for two reasons. One, because of the second initial "O". Walter Billington had no middle name. And two, because in the census of 1881 he was listed as a "woollen warehouseman" rather (unless he thereafter changed his job) than anything connected with the stage. So was he related to Fred in any other way? If he was, I've found no evidence of it. Apart from his presence in D'Oyly Carte cricket teams – not that, as a cricketer, he was anything special – nothing is known about him. He may have been a chorister. Or he may not have been a performer at all but, say, a Company baggage or props master. The jury, if not the umpires, are out on that one.

And while we're on the subject of Billingtons other than Fred, what of the rest of his family? Thomas, his father, had died in 1860 at the age of forty. Presumably in consequence of this, and in order to support her still young family, Sarah, his mother, had taken up millinery, and by 1871 had her own mother living with them. As for her three other sons, though, they each in turn disappeared into oblivion, and in oblivion they remained, at any rate so far as Fred himself was concerned.

It seems fairly likely that, once established in D'Oyly Carte, he (Fred) simply lost touch with them all, and lost interest in them too, for it's doubtful whether he ever spoke of them to any of his D'Oyly Carte colleagues. So little about them was known, indeed, that when he died the only light anyone could throw on their whereabouts or even existence was the suggestion that he had a brother in America.

Given all this, therefore, it also seems likely that he even stayed in a hotel during the D'Oyly Carte seasons he played down the years in Huddersfield itself. In all there were ten of these: three in the 1880s and the rest between 1894 and 1901. It would be too much to expect any evidence to turn up showing which of Huddersfield's hotels he patronised on any of these occasions. But here are four possibilities listed in the town's Directory and Yearbook of 1881 and 1887, along with an indication in three cases of what they advertised as offering:

1. Cherry Tree Commercial Hotel, Westgate/Market Street.
2. Commercial Hotel and Dining Rooms, Market Walk. "Good commercial and smoke rooms etc."
3. Crown Hotel, Westgate. "Wines, spirits etc of the finest quality. Private families supplied. First class stabling etc."
4. Pack Horse Commercial Hotel, Kirkgate. "Wines and spirits of the choicest quality, bottled ale, stout and porter, cigars etc; an ordinary [that is, a set price] meal every day at one o'clock. Billiards; superior stabling etc."

It's not, I hope, taking speculation too far to suggest that the last mentioned of these would most likely have gone furthest to satisfy a man with a gargantuan appetite and a strong penchant for cigars.

And after all that it seems appropriate to round off this chapter with another Billington anecdote centring on a hotel, and an anecdote told this time by himself:

"Once when I was staying in a hotel at Oban in Scotland, a crowd of people gathered in front of the building who eyed me curiously every time I went in or came out. Surely, I thought at first, my fame hasn't penetrated as far as this! Eventually, though, the repeated attention to which I was being subjected became so damned annoying that I complained to the hotel management, and the reason for the presence of the staring crowd quickly became clear. It was the hotel 'boots' who had put them up to it.

'It's all right, sir,' said this damned young scamp. 'It was a lark. I told them you was Billington the hangman'."

James Billington, like W.O. no relation, whose career in the latter capacity spanned the years 1884 to 1901, began it, ironically enough, as the "Yorkshire Hangman". Ah well, if nothing else, it makes an intriguing footnote.

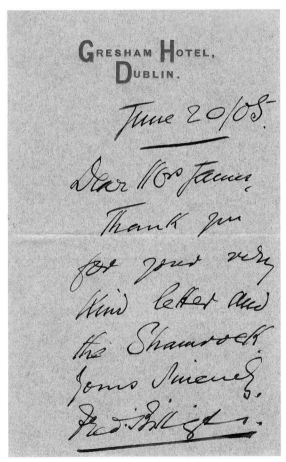

A letter written by Billington from Dublin's Gresham Hotel
(Author's collection)

"He's gone Abroad", 1885-88

From the cast list of certain German *Mikado* programmes:

"Pooh-Bah (Collectivministerportefoulletonist): Mr Fred Billington"

["Collectivministerportefoulletonist" – literally "Collective Minister Portfolio-Holder", or even, more idiomatically, "Minister with a Whole Collection of Portfolios"]

Saturday, August 8th 1885.
The place was Liverpool docks; the time eight o'clock in the morning. A party of forty or fifty people were being transported in a tender or passenger boat out to a large Cunard liner, the *SS Aurania*, anchored a short distance nearer the open sea in readiness for its latest voyage to America.

The party, the leader of which appeared to be a Mr Harry Chapman, was composed of both sexes in roughly equal numbers. There was about them a scarcely concealed excitement, almost as though they were a group of children being taken on an unexpected outing.

The passenger boat reached the liner, and the party transferred themselves to the liner with the minimum of fuss. Once aboard they spent time exploring the big ship or simply relaxing, according to taste, until just after three o'clock in the afternoon when the passenger boat approached the ship once more. This time it was bringing out the rest of the passengers, more than three hundred of them, who were to make the voyage. Its reappearance, indeed, had been expected, and the moment it was spotted the first party broke up, vanishing, every one of them, into their various cabins and locking the doors behind them.

And there in their cabins they stayed until the liner weighed anchor and the voyage had indisputably begun. Gradually now they emerged until eventually, at dinner, they were all together again, the undercurrent of excitement they exuded being, if anything, even more marked than before. Anybody who listened to any of their conversations closely, or heard them addressing any of the stewards, was likely to have become aware how much they stressed each other's names. Those names, besides Mr Chapman, included a Mr Hurley, a Mr Donn and a Mr Clarke – all unremarkable names, as it might be thought – and a Miss Caddy, a "Miss T. Caddy", apparently, a name that by contrast was remarkable in more ways than one.

The meal over and the day drawing to a close, they all returned to their respective cabins. And in their cabins they once again remained, not just overnight, but for the start of the following morning too, while the ship docked for a short time at Queenstown (now Cobh) in the south of Ireland.

But then, after they left Queenstown and were back on the open sea, they once more emerged – and this time as their true selves. Mr Harry Chapman, it was now discovered, was none other than Richard D'Oyly Carte; and the party itself, every member of which had been registered for the voyage under a false name, was one of his companies on its way to perform in New York.

It was one of the biggest adventures in D'Oyly Carte history. But what was it all about? Why the false names? Why all the secrecy? The answer had to do with the opera they were to play when they arrived: *The Mikado*.

The Mikado, Gilbert and Sullivan's successor to *Princess Ida*, had opened in London at the Savoy Theatre on March 14th that year, and it soon became clear that even by G&S standards it was something special. Its huge box office potential was quickly recognised by certain American theatre managers, and two of the latter soon made contact with Carte about the possibility of a New York production. One of these was a man named James C. Duff; the other had the unmistakably American name of John Stetson.

It was a case of instant rivalry. What both men were after was an agreement with Carte to present the "authorised" production of the opera. Stetson was the one who succeeded in getting the necessary go-ahead, and that should have been that.

But Duff, having failed in his own bid largely through demanding excessively favourable terms, had no intention of taking his failure lying down. He openly announced that he would mount a rival production of *The Mikado*, and that there was nothing in American copyright law to stop him doing so. He planned to open this rival production in mid-August, and immediately Carte decided he was going to upstage him.

Upstaging him meant arranging with Stetson to get the authorised production put on first. It meant transporting to America a Company of his own, and a fully rehearsed Company too. Not only that, but he had to do it speedily – and he had to do it as an undercover operation to prevent Duff getting wind of what was happening and speeding up the preparations for *his* production in consequence. One of the performers Carte chose for this purpose was Fred Billington, who would play Rutland Barrington's part of Pooh-Bah.

Billington first played Pooh-Bah for Carte's "D" Company at the Theatre Royal, Brighton during the week beginning July 27th, and it can be said straight away that it would in time become his most famous part, the part by which, more than any other, most people who saw him on stage remembered him. His performance that July evening in Brighton, though, gained only qualified praise from the reviewer who covered the production for the *Brighton Gazette*:

"Mr Fred Billington as Pooh-Bah, who is described as 'Lord High Everything Else'," he wrote, "has fewer opportunities of shining" – fewer opportunities of shining, that is, than Ko-Ko. But as I've suggested previously, that was the way the two parts were written, and the comment wasn't necessarily to Billington's discredit. Pooh-Bah is arguably one of the hardest G&S parts for an actor to "get into". Rutland Barrington himself claimed to have found it so. As he (Barrington) explained:

> "During rehearsals it was evident to me that Gilbert was not quite satisfied with my rendering of Pooh-Bah, and it worried me considerably, because I could not quite make out what he wanted. I naturally tried my hardest to fall in with his wishes and things seemed a little better, but when I said to him after some fortnight's work, 'I hope that is more what you want,' his reply came as rather a shock. 'My dear Barrington, I have no doubt it will be an admirable performance, but it is no more my idea of Pooh-Bah than chalk is like cheese.'
>
> I then suggested that possibly a quiet visit paid to him at home, coupled with an hour or two's devotion to the exposition of his views, might have the desired effect. This was duly carried out, and as Gilbert afterwards said, the upshot was a performance that exactly embodied his idea of the part. My recompense came at the end of the first performance, when he came to my dressing room … and thanked me for 'my invaluable aid to the success of the piece'."

H'm.

Back to the American trip.

On the Sunday at the end of their Brighton week, Fred Billington and the rest of "D" Company travelled to Liverpool to begin what was announced as a fortnight's season at the Lancashire city's Royal Court Theatre. The first five nights, Monday to Friday, were played with the advertised cast. But that Friday, August 7th, those members of the Company chosen to go to America received instructions for the Saturday.

George Thorne, the performer who was to play Ko-Ko in America, described what happened, at least in his own case, in a later book of reminiscences. On the Wednesday – that is, just two days earlier – Richard D'Oyly Carte had turned up in Liverpool and had asked him if he could leave for America in a hurry. Says Thorne:

> "I replied: 'Yes.'

He asked: 'How soon?'

I answered: 'Tomorrow, if you wish'."

Then on the Friday night he received a telegram: "Meet Company Lime Street six a.m. tomorrow, special train; proceed to Angel Hotel for breakfast; from there to *SS Aurania* by special tender at eight a.m."

Which is where we came in.

Was the Angel Hotel chosen because of its position, which was not far from the docks? Was it even the hotel in which Fred Billington was staying for the Liverpool visit? Either way, the America-bound members of the Company duly had breakfast there that Saturday morning. All of them had been sworn to total secrecy about what was happening, and all of them prepared from then on to use their false names.

So, with regard to those false names, who was who? Harry Chapman, as already mentioned, was Richard D'Oyly Carte. Mr Hurley – "Fred" Hurley – was George Thorne. Mr Donn – "Felix" Donn – was Courtice Pounds, the principal tenor, who was to play Nanki-Poo. The improbable Miss T. Caddy was the vivacious Company soubrette, Kate Forster, who was to play Pitti-Sing. Mr Clarke – Mr "E" Clarke, whatever the "E" was intended to stand for – was Fred Billington. And now, breakfast finished, the party got themselves to the landing-stage to board the tender that was to take them out to the *Aurania*.

If the reason for their assuming false names, as for all the rest of the secrecy, was simple, so was the reason why they felt able to revert to their real names once the *Aurania* was away from Queenstown. Queenstown was the ship's only port of call *en route*. The next port of call was New York itself. Now nobody could spill the beans and pass on their whereabouts because the technology at that time was insufficiently advanced for any cables – the only possible means of communication – to be sent from a vessel at sea on or back to shore, whether "shore" was New York or anywhere else.

Now they were free to enjoy what George Thorne called "all the usual amusements to be got out of a life on board ship". On the Friday, the sixth day of the voyage, they gave a concert. The items they sang were a mixture of G&S and non-G&S. Billington himself sang Dr Daly's first song from *The Sorcerer*, and joined the rest of the Company in "I hear the soft note" from *Patience*. Courtice Pounds sang one of the top Victorian pops, "Come into the garden, Maud", and Kate Forster sang another Victorian song, "Dearer all to me", this last a song composed by another member of the Company, Frederick Federici. In the concert Federici (real name Frederick Baker) acted as accompanist for the song. In New York he was to play *The Mikado's* title-role.

The concert, like all ship's concerts, helped to pass the time, and also helped in this case to keep the lid on the Company's mounting excitement as, at last, the liner neared the American coast. Had all the planning and secrecy worked, or had the news of their voyage somehow leaked out? The answer came when they docked on the Sunday or Monday. No one had known anything until someone back in England had alerted New York when they were halfway across, and by then it was too late to matter. They were there. They had arrived. Now it was a case of getting their production ready for opening.

Moreover speed was still of the essence, for James Duff, they immediately discovered, had announced the opening of his rival production for the Wednesday, August 19th, just hours ahead. Carte and Stetson promptly decided they would open *their* production the same night. The newspapers revelled in the situation. They referred to the Stetson-Duff rivalry as war. And it quickly became clear who was winning the war. Duff was unsettled. He announced a postponement of his production first till the Thursday, then till the following Monday.

For five days, therefore, Carte and Stetson had the field to themselves. Their production – the authentic D'Oyly Carte production – duly opened at Stetson's Fifth Avenue Theatre on the Wednesday night.

It was one of those opening nights that could hardly have gone better. A packed house, a rapturous reception and, in the days that followed, glowing reviews and press coverage. Everything about the production was praised: the libretto, the music, the chorus work, the team spirit, the costumes, the stage business, the colour, slickness and vitality of the whole performance.

And when it came to the individual members of the cast it was the same. There was one disappointment: Geraldine Ulmar, later to be a leading light at the Savoy, and who was making her G&S debut as Yum-Yum, was criticised for the less than satisfactory delivery of her dialogue. But against that, four of the rest were instantly hailed as stars; and first of those four – unsurprisingly, given the part he was playing – was George Thorne. "It was reserved for Mr Thorne," wrote the New York correspondent of the *Era*, "to make the hit of the evening. His dry humour, clear enunciation and agility at once put him high up in public favour."

Second on the list – likewise unsurprisingly – was Courtice Pounds, the first D'Oyly Carte tenor to have any real sex appeal and romantic glamour about him. As Nanki-Poo "his bright, fresh appearance was a delight to the audience, and it was a pleasure to hear his tuneful voice," declared the same correspondent; though it was his comic duet in the second act with Thorne, "The Flowers that bloom in the spring", that brought the most delirious audience response where he was concerned. "The Flowers that bloom in the spring" had been second only to the "Three Little Maids" trio in the response it had evoked on *The Mikado's* first night in London. It was the same in New York, and would generally be the same elsewhere.

Third of the instant stars – unsurprisingly again – was Frederick Federici in the title-role; and fourth, which *was* surprising, was Kate Forster as Pitti-Sing – surprising because Pitti-Sing is really only a secondary part. If Courtice Pounds quickly became the idol of scores of New York young ladies (and he acquired the soubriquet "vest pocket tenor" to prove it) Kate Forster had the same effect upon New York's young men:

"The Japanese graces of Miss Foster [*sic*] have been telegraphed and written all over the country" (wrote the *Era* correspondent a fortnight later). "She is simply delightful in the part. The more impressionable portion of New York compares her to a poem, a mosaic, a dream of exquisite loveliness.

Billington as Pooh-Bah and George Thorne as Ko-Ko, New York, 1885
(Author's collection)

This part of New York pays to go and see her nightly. They are pleased; so must be Miss Foster ..."

But where in all this was Fred Billington? Obviously he was never going to be a dream of exquisite loveliness himself. Yet wasn't he – as Pooh-Bah – one of the main stars of the show too?

Strangely the answer is "apparently not". "Mr F. Billington's Pooh-Bah," declared the reviewer who covered the first night for the *New York Times*, was "remarkable for consistent and fairly comical dignity", but was "not flavoured with very communicative drollery" – which was qualified praise at best, and matched the similarly qualified praise his playing of the character had received in Brighton. Though he was in New York for the full duration of the D'Oyly Carte visit, he seems to have attracted peculiarly little specific attention.

Yet perhaps that's not an entirely fair assessment, for he undoubtedly made a strong impact here and there. On Monday August 24th James Duff's rival *Mikado* opened. It had its strong points – notably that certain of the principals were considered better singers than their D'Oyly Carte counterparts. But overall, and particularly visually, it was not a success. Carte and Stetson had won the war conclusively.

And in the wake of this, the correspondent who reviewed Duff's production for the *Era* indulged in some fantasy casting. Taking the Carte-Stetson production, Duff's production, and another unauthorised production which was now showing its face, he asked himself who in the three productions had proved the best player in each part. For answer he chose, surprisingly, just the Peep-Bo from Duff's production; the Ko-Ko, Yum-Yum and Katisha from the other unauthorised production; and, from Carte's production, Kate Forster, Courtice Pounds and Frederick Federici as, respectively, the best Pitti-Sing, Nanki-Poo and Mikado – and Fred Billington as the best Pooh-Bah.

And two other references to Billington's performance of Pooh-Bah in New York must also be mentioned. One of these was from an unspecified press review quoted from memory by George Thorne:

"The principal comedian, George Thorne, is as funny as a section of gas pipe, while Messrs Byron Browne and Fred Billington are two solemn imbeciles."

George Byron Browne played Pish-Tush for the tour's first five months.

That "imbecile" comment can simply be laughed off. But fortunately the other reference to Billington was more significant, a comment made many years later by the man himself. Referring to the New York audiences, he remarked: "I'm thankful to say I got on very well with them. Pooh-Bah was quite to their liking."

"*The Mikado* at the Fifth Avenue Theatre is really doing an astounding business," reported an *Era* correspondent on September 3rd. "Hundreds nightly seek admission, only to find there is no room for them." As was the case with the Japanese opera in London, the D'Oyly Carte production in New York went

Billington pictured as Pooh-Bah on one of the many "trade cards" spawned by
the 1885-86 New York *Mikado* visit
(Collection: Katie Barnes)

on and on. On September 24th it notched its fiftieth performance – a gala performance conducted by Sullivan himself. In due course it reached its hundredth performance, its hundred and fiftieth, its two hundredth, and didn't close till it had given performance number two hundred and two.

The date of that closing performance was May 8th the following year (1886), and the same night or the next day Fred Billington and the rest of the Company boarded another Cunard liner – quite openly; there was no need of any secrecy now – for the voyage back to England. They had been away more than nine months.

So was that the end of their foreign travels? The answer for most of them was "no, anything but". After just a couple of dates (Liverpool and Manchester) at home, they were off again. On May 29th the *Era* was reporting this new departure:

> "Mr D'Oyly Carte's American *Mikado* Company leave Manchester tonight (Saturday) by [the] Midland Railway, *en route* to Berlin via Queenborough and Flushing, the arrangements for their transit being entrusted to Mr John Bosworth of the Midland Company in conjunction with Messrs Thomas Cook and Son."

Arriving in Berlin on June 1st, the D'Oyly Carters had a hurried rehearsal the following morning, and gave the opening performance of what was to be a tour of Germany and Austria the same evening.

Taking *The Mikado* to Germany. It was one thing to take G&S to America. Americans, after all, speak English. It was quite another to take it anywhere in Continental Europe, where English was *not* the first language. The English language in Berlin, wrote one local critic, "has hitherto been oftener heard in the drawing room than on the stage". What would German audiences make of it – not just a production in English but an English comic opera at that?

The question was answered straight away by that first Berlin performance. They loved it. They might not have understood half of Gilbert's allusions. They might have missed any number of verbal points. But the plot of *The Mikado,* insofar as it matters, is surely not too difficult to get the gist of even in a foreign language. And there was no question about the pleasure they took in the music, while the brilliance of the production that had so delighted New York proved irresistible here too. Between the acts that first night, according to the critic quoted above, "one overheard such remarks as 'Very original', 'Unique' and even 'Grossartig', which may be rendered 'Magnificent'." And all this set the tone for the tour as a whole.

(As well as *The Mikado*, it needs to be said, the Company at different times during the tour added *Trial by Jury* to the bill, playing it as a curtain-raiser – which, given that *The Mikado* is hardly one of the shortest G&S operas, and especially so when encores are taken into account, must have meant a pretty long evening for all concerned.)

In Berlin the Company played a season of four weeks, then moved on to seasons of varying lengths in other towns, among them Hamburg, Dresden,

Breslau, Leipzig, Vienna and Stuttgart, finishing with a return visit to Berlin in December and the beginning of January. The only alteration to their programme came between their sojourns in Vienna and Stuttgart, when they were booked to go to Budapest, but cancelled the visit because of an outbreak of cholera there and simply extended their Vienna season instead.

The cast throughout the tour remained the same as had played *The Mikado* in New York, with just two exceptions. Geraldine Ulmar, who as Yum-Yum had fully redeemed herself in the American city after her less than satisfactory start, was replaced in Germany after a month by a newcomer to the part, Clara Merivale. ("With a light but exceedingly interesting voice," the latter "riveted attention as much by her singing as by her acting," wrote a critic in Leipzig.) David Fisher, who had been Carte's first choice for New York, but who almost at the last minute had backed out of the American visit, was now apparently happy to go to Germany, and replaced George Thorne as Ko-Ko.

As Ko-Ko he duly became the most popular member of the Company. He "took advantage of" the double encore given for "The Flowers that bloom in the spring", wrote that same Leipzig critic, to put in "fresh features of comicality" – though his tour was spoilt when he went down with illness in Vienna. Courtice Pounds repeated the triumph he had achieved in America as Nanki-Poo.

And Frederick Federici repeated his American triumph likewise, while adding further to his laurels on the last night of the first Berlin season. At the end of the performance the performers were presented by members of the audience with bouquets of flowers. The largest of these was presented to Federici in his persona as the Mikado himself, and he felt it incumbent on him to say a few words of thanks on behalf of them all. Which he duly did – in German.

But where, once again, was Fred Billington in all this? Would *he* have attempted in such circumstances to make a speech in German? He might well have had a go, though it's not so easy to imagine him accepting an immense floral tribute with the easy graciousness that Federici managed. Still, that's of no great significance. What *was* significant was the fact that he didn't feature specially prominently in the tour notices. In certain reviews, indeed, he wasn't mentioned at all. As in New York, or so it seemed, he was only considered to be among the second rank of principals.

Nonetheless he wasn't slow to form impressions of Germany and the German theatrical scene. In referring to those impressions, though, it needs to be said that he was to take part in a second D'Oyly Carte Continental tour two years later (see pages 56-7) and it's not always clear which of the tours he was talking about. One thing that continually struck him was the high standard of the German theatre orchestras, particularly when compared with the orchestras he had encountered and would continue to encounter in the provinces at home:

"On the Continent the orchestras everywhere were magnificent, numbering never less than forty, sometimes as many as eighty, and all excellent players.

49

The inadequacy of our English provincial orchestras is terrible. Only the most hardened artist can witness, unmoved, the murder of Sullivan's scores, when twenty instruments have to do the work of sixty or seventy.

Our native instrumentalists may be, doubtless they are, individually as proficient as the foreigners, but to compare the numerical strength of an ordinary English provincial orchestra with those found even in second or third-class German theatres is as unfair as it is absurd, seeing that in Germany theatre bands are subsidised by Government."

Government, or at any rate officialdom, he would explain, also featured prominently when it came to theatrical safety. Once when asked "Which country in your opinion has the best theatres?" he answered:

"Well, if you mean from the point of view of comfort, they vary greatly in each country. But Germany's theatres, I should say, are the safest … All through the Continent our scenery had to be specially prepared. A bit of scenery anywhere would be cut out and tested by the local authorities, who would afterwards stamp on it 'Diese Materialien sind ganz feuerfest gemacht'."

At a time when devastating theatre fires were all too prevalent, this was "health and safety" applied to real purpose; and it was something also commented on in print by another member of the Continental *Mikado* Company. A month or so after their initial arrival in Berlin, one of the "Three Little Maids" took it into her head to write an occasional letter to the editor of the *Era* giving him – and when those letters were published, the paper's readers – quite lengthy accounts and descriptions of the progress of the tour. From internal evidence in the letters themselves the writer must have been either Geraldine St Maur (Peep-Bo) or, probably more likely, Kate Forster (Pitti-Sing), as whichever of them it was simply signed herself "One of the Three Little Maids" each time.

Anyhow on the question of the scenery, the Little Maid, whichever she was, commented that, having arrived in Vienna,

"We went to hear Strauss at the Volksgarten the second evening we were here, as we did not play the first two nights, the authorities making us have all our scenery repainted with fireproof paints."

She also reported on the inadequacies of the Viennese drainage system and on what turned out to be a distinctly un-blue Danube.

Curiously, though this was obviously deliberate, she didn't once in these letters mention by name any of her fellow performers, and those fellow performers of course included Billington. But she may well have been thinking of Billington when, in her first letter of all, she got on to the subject of food:

"You would have laughed to have seen some of our Company when we first came over eyeing the meats etc which were placed before us at meals at the hotel in Berlin.

They could not swallow the raw ham, protesting that we were not cannibals, and looked askance at the cold veal and sausages, though most of them have taken very kindly since to the latter."

And reverting to their time in Vienna, I can't leave a mention of these letters without including her account of an incident that happened while they were there. Imagine that the names of the people involved were Yum-Yum, Peep-Bo, Pitti-Sing and Pooh-Bah, and it could have been an incident straight out of *The Mikado* itself:

"We had rather an amusing adventure just before leaving the Austrian capital, the 'Three Little Maids' being on the point of imprisonment for insulting the officer who represented the fire brigade in the theatre, and who had stationed himself in one of the wings in such a manner that the artists could not pass him in their exits and entrances.

He was very angry with us because, after repeated remonstrances with him, we all three trotted down to him and giggled at him from behind our fans to annoy him, and he declared we had insulted him grossly, and he actually lodged a complaint against us with the police.

It really threatened to become serious when Mr Carte's representative was called down to the police office, and was told that we were liable to be locked up for insulting an officer while in discharge of his duty.

However, this gentleman having suggested that the 'Three Little Maids' should come down and kiss the irate and injured officer and so make peace with him, the case was dismissed, with laughter."

"What do you want me to do to them?" demands Pooh-Bah in the opera. "Mind, I will not kiss them."

But the last word on the Continental tours for the moment must come not from Pooh-Bah but from Fred Billington himself. And the last word in question relates not to kissing but to something potentially more serious. In a press interview several years later he apparently said something on the lines of having in his time had

"some remarkable experiences, including a duel on the Continent, the results of which were by no means like those of certain French duels."

Did he really fight a duel? Or even a pretend duel with (say) stage swords or maybe unloaded pistols such as are mentioned in *Cox and Box*? Sadly it seems impossible to say. For apart from that one mention I've found no reference to the subject anywhere.

The Company arrived back in England early in January (1887), but once again, as when they returned from America, they didn't stay back in England for long. By mid-February they were off abroad again, making a return visit to New York. This time they were going there to play *Ruddigore*.

The London run of *The Mikado* had at last come to an end on January 19th. *Ruddigore*, its successor, took over at the Savoy three days later, and already Richard D'Oyly Carte had publicly intimated that he'd be sending a Company to play it in America. This time, furthermore, he was doing so within weeks of the London opening rather than months, as had been the case with *The Mikado*. This time there was no threat of prior or rival productions, so this time there was no subterfuge involved.

This time, too, he even had the New York Company giving two matinee performances of *Ruddigore* at the Savoy itself (February 9th and 10th) before they set off. As a Company, wrote an *Era* reporter who attended one of these matinees, they were very efficient. And who, in the opinion of that reporter, were the stars? He named four names: Geraldine Ulmar, back once more in place of Clara Merivale; Kate Forster; Frederick Federici; and Courtice Pounds. But, strangely, not George Thorne, once more replacing David Fisher for an American visit. And not Fred Billington either, even though Billington was cast as Sir Despard – a part which, as previously suggested, gives the performer a particularly strong chance to shine. Was this yet again a case of Billington being relegated, even if unintentionally, to the second rank of principals?

That was one question. And there was another question too, this one concerning *Ruddigore* itself. The new opera had received what might be described as a mixed reception in London, and this was known about in America before the Company arrived in New York. So how would *Ruddigore* be received there? The date of its New York opening was February 21st. The theatre was again the Fifth Avenue Theatre, the venue of the unalloyed triumph of *The Mikado* not so many months before; and for the first half hour or so of the performance it looked as though *Ruddigore* was heading for a similar triumph.

The audience, packing the theatre in every part, was (wrote the reviewer from the *New York Times*) "unquestionably in a friendly mood". The overture was enthusiastically applauded, the first seven or eight numbers in Act One scarcely less so. The principals, all remembered for their performances in *The Mikado*, and all thought of as old friends, were each welcomed with "prolonged demonstrations of pleasure" on their first entrances.

But then the mood began to change. Somehow everyone on stage was giving the appearance of being nervous and ill at ease; a condition which, the *Times* noted, was soon affecting the watchers too. "After the first half of the first act there was a palpable diminution of interest on the part of the audience, and it must be frankly admitted that there were periods in the course of the evening when people were bored."

It was an almost identical repeat of what had happened on *Ruddigore's* first night at the Savoy. Most of the first act that night had gone with the characteristic G&S swing, but during the second act a sense of disappointment seemed to infect the audience, leading ultimately to calls from the gallery to

Billington as Sir Despard, New York, 1887
(Collection: David Stone)

"Give us back *The Mikado*". The New York audience didn't go as far as that. But there was no doubt that, as part of the heading to the *Times* review put it, *Ruddigore* in the city was "not a hit".

And the sense of disappointment that affected the first night never fully went away. The opera in New York notched only forty-five performances, less than a quarter of the number *The Mikado* had achieved. By the end of April the Company were back in Britain once more, and the personnel involved, the majority of whom had been together getting on for two years, dispersed.

But for Billington at least, it wasn't quite a case of saying goodbye to *Ruddigore* altogether. The opera was still being played at the Savoy, and was also now being played by two of D'Oyly Carte's provincial touring companies. Fred Billington was duly drafted into "B" Company, and beefing up its performances by his portrayal of Sir Despard in a way he had never quite managed to do in New York.

From the *Salisbury Journal*, July 16th:

"In the second act one of the funniest things in the whole opera is the duet between the ex-Sir Despard (Mr F. Billington), changed into the most sedate of men, with long hair, a big green umbrella, and an aspect of the severest respectability, and Mad Margaret, mad no longer, but the primmest of all possible maidens (except when she forgets herself) in a poke bonnet projecting beyond her face.

'I once was a very abandoned person', the duet begins, and good as the singing is, the dance is better. The extreme gravity with which the exercise is conducted at the end of each verse is not to be described, but it is one of the drollest things conceivable."

The Mad Margaret on this occasion was Haidee Crofton, who had played Hebe in the *Pinafore* Company in which Billington had made his D'Oyly Carte debut back in 1879.

The dancing and stage business that form an integral part of the duet always pose potential hazards to the performers. And in one performance that August the Margaret and Despard of Carte's "C" Company (Kate Forster and George Temple) came a real cropper, as the *Era* reported with some glee:

"During the performance of the second act of *Ruddigore* at the Theatre Royal, Hull on Tuesday evening a ludicrous incident occurred. Sir Despard and Margaret having responded to [calls for] an encore for their duet, repeated the 'business' at the end. Sir Despard had scarcely uttered the line 'This sort of thing takes a deal of training' when both overbalanced themselves and fell sprawling on the stage. Of course the audience laughed uproariously."

Don't you love that "of course"?

Billington's appearances as Sir Despard in Britain, though, were not confined to the provinces. As well as taking part in those two matinees given by the New York Company, he also played the part at the Savoy for a week that

Billington as Sir Despard, with Kate Forster as Mad Margaret, New York, 1887
(Collection: David Stone)

August in place of Rutland Barrington. Officially that week Barrington was away on holiday – or, as Billington referred to it, "golfing". Of which more anon.

"Mr H.M. Imano has returned to England after a most successful tour on the Continent with Mr R. D'Oyly Carte's Opera Company," recorded the *Era* three months later. It was a brief item of news, the sort of item the paper carried each week. So what was its significance?

The key phrase was "the Continent". The success of the first D'Oyly Carte Continental tour had encouraged Carte to arrange a second such tour. That second tour had begun in April (1887) and this time took in venues not only in Germany and Austria but in Denmark and Holland as well. This time, too, a largely different set of performers was involved; and among those not included in their ranks was Fred Billington who, like several others, was expected to be away in America with *Ruddigore* during much of the relevant period. That being the case, various substitute performers were needed, and Billington's place was taken by Henry Imano, a performer who had only joined D'Oyly Carte the previous December, and who was now, as that news item indicated, leaving the tour.

His going at this point may well have been fixed some time in advance. But whether it had been or not, it got Billington participating in that second Continental tour after all, as the performer chosen to be *his* replacement in turn. As Billington himself later put it:

> "I remember playing … at Leicester on a Friday night, and on the Sunday following I was Pooh-Bah in Amsterdam."

The date of that Amsterdam performance was November 6th. And having arrived on the Continent he stayed there till the tour came to an end the following February.

In most respects this second tour was similar to its predecessor. But one respect in which it was somewhat different concerned its repertoire. *The Mikado* was again on the bill, though not *Trial by Jury*. But this time the bill also included two more of the full-length operas, *HMS Pinafore* and *Patience*. *The Mikado* in its customary fashion once again carried all before it. *Patience*, though, was an unlikely choice for such a tour, and didn't fully justify its presence; while even *Pinafore*, an opera hugely popular in America, was not quite the success it might have been. Clearly the German public didn't fully understand it. To take just one aspect of this:

> "Such a specimen of a man-o'-war sailor as Dick Deadeye, the press remarked" (and as Fred Billington, the Deadeye in question, explained sardonically) "would never be admitted into the German Imperial Navy"

and he had a no less sardonic comment to make on the earlier German response to *Trial by Jury*:

"If *Trial by Jury* was a sample of English law proceedings, they preferred their own methods."

He also had comments to make on the German audiences he encountered on the two Continental tours. Many of these audiences – not that he mentioned this in so many words – were "fashionable" – fashionable, indeed, to an extraordinary extent – and the number of performances at which they included Royalty was almost too many to count. This was European and petty German Royalty at its most ostentatious and homogeneous. Even so, it was quite something when, at a performance of *The Mikado* in Copenhagen a few weeks before Billington joined the Company on the second tour, the audience included the King and Queen of Denmark, the King and Queen of Greece, the Czar and Czarina of Russia and the Prince and Princess of Wales.

The only representatives of European Royalty before whom Billington himself played, however, were members of the various German branches - though these included not one but two future Kaisers, Friedrich and Wilhelm. Friedrich, the first of these, took to *The Mikado* in a way that left no room for doubt, and went to see the Japanese opera several times. According to an *Era* correspondent writing towards the end of the first tour, he had been "so delighted with the previous performances of the Company in Berlin that he … engaged a private box capable of holding eight persons for the whole five weeks of the Company's [second] stay".

Nor was this all. For he was also, according to one of Billington's obituarists, a not infrequent visitor to the actor's dressing room when the Company were in the German capital.

But what was the future Kaiser Friedrich's favourite number in *The Mikado*? The answer was the Pooh-Bah, Ko-Ko, Pish-Tush trio in Act One, to which he would apparently refer not by its first line "I am so proud" but as "The Cheap and chippy chopper" song, and for which, says Billington, he also, when in the audience, demanded an encore.

And no doubt, given who he was, he always got one.

"Elephantine in Drollery", 1888-95

"Fred Billington, when playing Pooh-Bah ... used to say on receipt of a number of presumably Japanese coins ... as a bribe: 'Another insult, and I think (*weighing them*) a light one – *Two D*.' The addition of the slang expression, though causing a laugh, utterly spoilt the Gilbertian pun on the word 'light'."

(Broughton "Virgilius" Black, a member of D'Oyly Carte, 1890, in the *Gilbert & Sullivan Journal,* October 1925)

Yes, but what *was* the Gilbertian pun on the word "light"? And where did that expression *Two D* come from?

It was now mid-1888. Billington was coming up to thirty-four and had been with D'Oyly Carte close on nine years. For the moment his foreign excursions were at an end, and he was back to full-time touring around the British Isles.

How can we describe his position in D'Oyly Carte at this time? As a "star" – that is, a theatrical "draw" - in himself? Perhaps surprisingly, given his eventual reputation, the answer to that question has to be "no". Taking those first nine years of his D'Oyly Carte career on their own, it is hard to make a case for him as being anything special. A competent performer, yes. A reliable performer, definitely. But that was as far as it went. Somehow he had yet to put a truly individual stamp on the parts he played.

One reason for this may lie in the fact that he was not yet fully associated with any one set of parts. At different times during 1888 "C" Company, the

Company to which, following his foreign excursions, he was now attached, performed five of the G&S operas: *HMS Pinafore*, *The Pirates of Penzance*, *Patience*, *The Mikado* and, from November, the latest in the series, *The Yeomen of the Guard*. And of the five parts he was to play in those operas that year, still only two – the Sergeant of Police and Pooh-Bah – were "Barrington" parts. The other three – that is, more than half – were "Richard Temple" parts: Dick Deadeye, Colonel Calverley in *Patience*, a part he'd also played on the Continent and a few weeks before that – the first time, indeed, that he'd played in *Patience* at all; and Sergeant Meryll, which was the first part he would play in *The Yeomen of the Guard*.

But there were signs that, in terms of his D'Oyly Carte profile, things might now be changing, that proper recognition of his talents might be coming at last. The fact that it was he who was chosen to replace Henry Imano in the Continental Company, rather than any other actual or potential Pooh-Bah around at the time, was perhaps one of those signs. Another was an increasing sense in his notices that he was now a performer of some substance. Here are two of these notices from that year relating to *Patience* and his portrayal of Colonel Calverley:

> "Mr F. Billington, a native of Huddersfield … gave an excellent rendering of the part of Colonel Calverley, his singing gaining him great applause."
>
> (*Huddersfield Daily Chronicle*)

> "Mr Fred Billington, another very able and important member of Mr D'Oyly Carte's Company, whose performances here on previous occasions are remembered with intense delight, makes a dashing representative of Colonel Calverley, one of the Dragoon officers. His robust voice and clear enunciation have never been heard in Bristol to greater advantage than in the popular song 'When I first put this uniform on' and in the choruses of the Dragoons."
>
> (*Bristol Times and Mirror*)

No question now of his being "a bit too stiff", as the same paper had described his Dr Daly seven years earlier (see page 28).

Given the impressive way in which he was playing the one soldier, Colonel Calverley, it was fairly logical that, when it came to *The Yeomen of the Guard*, he should be cast as the ex-soldier Sergeant Meryll. "Mr Fred Billington is … happily suited in the part of Sergeant Meryll," wrote the local *Era* correspondent of the Company's first performance of *Yeomen* in Manchester; and here are the equivalent comments made during the months that followed by five other local *Era* correspondents, each of them finding a slightly different way of saying the same thing:

> "Mr Fred Billington was seen to much advantage as the burly Sergeant Meryll."
>
> (Edinburgh)

"Mr Fred Billington was an excellent representative of Sergeant Meryll, and sang with much power."

(York)

"Old Meryll was admirably hit off by Mr Fred Billington."

(Nottingham)

"Mr Dan Billington [*sic*] is the bluff Sergeant."

(Bradford)

"Mr Fred Billington made a fine *vieux militaire*."   Mon mot!

(Dundee)

Despite all this, though, the strongest memory he himself had of playing Meryll was not the success he made of the part, but one of those stage contretemps that happen at times to all actors good and bad, and which all actors dread – and then dine out on.

"I was once" (he would explain) "playing Sergeant Meryll at the Court Theatre, Liverpool and was waiting for Colonel Fairfax, who has now disguised himself as Young Meryll, to come on. I had just said 'The Colonel comes' when I noticed that he *wasn't* coming – he was late. So I began to gag a bit, standing at the side from which he should have entered. 'But no, he has turned away – it will delay him', and so on, only for him to eventually appear on stage, because it was nearer for him, from the *other* side.

Well of course this made me look silly, and I felt so mad to think that after I had covered his non-appearance he should give me away like that, that I turned round and said 'You bloody fool!', heartily and evidently not *sotto voce*, because next day one of the Liverpool papers had it that 'Burly Fred Billington used words last night that were not written by Mr Gilbert. But he was perfectly justified in doing so'."

As to who was the bloody fool playing Fairfax on this occasion there are, going by the records, two possibilities, by name Lyn Cadwaladr and Charles Conyers. And perhaps it's best to leave it at that.

A third sign that Billington was gaining greater prominence came during the following year, 1889, and in this case there was no mistaking the significance of what happened. On May 25th David Fisher died, and in the wake of this Billington was asked to give up playing Sergeant Meryll and take on the part of Wilfred Shadbolt, which Fisher had been playing, instead.

As previously mentioned, Wilfred Shadbolt, the *Yeomen* head jailer, had been written as the equivalent of the opera's Barrington part. But the fact that it was created at the Savoy by W.H. Denny and on tour by Fisher made it initially a rather different part from the part it might have been had Barrington created it himself. Compared with Barrington Denny was slim, agile, much more alert-looking and much more an obvious comedian, while Fisher had made his name as an exponent of the "Grossmith" parts. And given the success they both made of Shadbolt, their lighter styles of performance might well have become the accepted – traditional – way of playing the part for evermore.

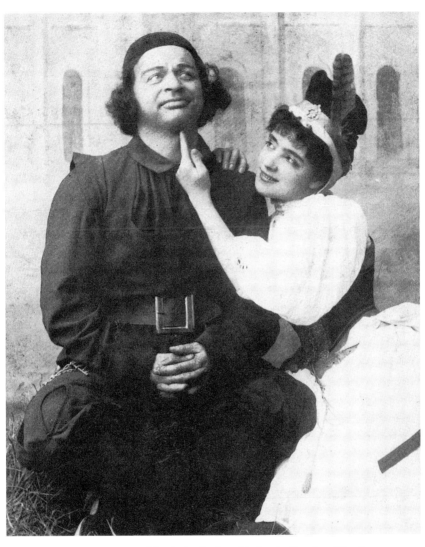

W.H. Denny as Wilfred Shadbolt, with Jessie Bond as Phoebe
(Collection: Tony Gower)

But the advent of Billington in the part put paid to this; and put paid to it not just temporarily but in effect permanently, at any rate where D'Oyly Carte casting was concerned. Instead the part came to be played more often than not by a heavier, older man, or at least a man some way past his youth; and there's a strong argument for saying that this had its less than satisfactory side, given that Shadbolt is, in his own way, part of the opera's love interest. As Audrey Williamson put it in her book *Gilbert & Sullivan Opera: a new assessment*, published in 1953:

> "Why should he always be played as middle-aged or older and the part allotted to the actor of Pooh-Bah? ... Surely Wilfred would seem a more possible suitor for Phoebe (who it appears had at one time encouraged him) if he were a younger man, loutish it is true, but fitting more naturally into the realistic plot ..."

It would have been interesting, she goes on, to see how a younger and, she could have added, slimmer man might have approached the part.

But instead there was "burly Fred Billington", now taking it on in his mid-thirties; and because "C" Company spent the entire year playing *Yeomen* exclusively, doing so for the next six or seven months at every performance. It was a part in which he totally revelled – to the extent that, from that time on, whenever anyone asked him the inevitable question "Which of your parts is your favourite?" he would answer "Shadbolt" without having to think about it for even half a second. "There's more character in the Jailer than many of the others," as he once put it. "He's a consistent chap all through the piece."

> "Never" (wrote one commentator) "will there be a Shadbolt so weirdly uncouth, so elephantine in drollery. To see poor Billington seated on the floor in the middle of the stage while Phoebe twits and torments, caresses and cozens him out of his keys, was only equalled by his massive gambols with Jack Point, bearing the jest book between them, when Shadbolt pursues his divine delusion that he is a born jester, and not a right goodly Chief [*sic*] Tormentor."
>
> (*Daily Mail*, Hull, 1917)

Shadbolt became one of what might be called his "defining" parts, along with Pooh-Bah, the part he would ultimately play more times than any other; the Sergeant of Police, the part he had been instrumental in creating; and Don Alhambra, the Grand Inquisitor in *The Gondoliers*, a part he would play for the first time early in the next year, 1890.

Immediately before and after New Year itself, however, there was a brief but curious interlude when, for whatever reason, he spent three weeks in Edinburgh playing in an American comic opera called *Paola* – the only time after 1879 that he appeared in a Company that did not bear the name of D'Oyly Carte.

Paola was set in Corsica around the year 1700, with a plot based on the trusty dramatic theme of a longstanding vendetta between two of the island's families. Billington played a suitably bloodthirsty character called Bragadoccio.

Billington as Don Alhambra, New York, 1890
(Collection: David Stone)

"Mr Fred Billington, a talented actor and effective singer, made a clever appearance as Bragadoccio, first ship-chandler and afterwards brigand," wrote the critic from the *Era*. "Mr Billington was a capital brigand," said the *Edinburgh Evening News*.

The production was also noteworthy for the presence in the cast of two other D'Oyly Carte performers. Leonora Braham, previously a star at the Savoy, played the title-role; while Fanny Harrison, a contralto who had been a leading light in the Carte touring companies, played a character with the wonderful name of Margarine.

Back to *The Gondoliers*.

The new G&S opera had opened in London to a glittering reception on December 7th. As with its predecessors, Richard D'Oyly Carte lost little time getting it into the repertoire of his provincial touring companies and arranging for it to be produced in New York. The New York production opened on January 7th 1890 – that is, exactly a month after the London opening – but expectation that it would be as successful in America as it was clearly going to be at home was immediately dashed. Its first night proved even less successful and more disappointing than the New York first night of *Ruddigore* had been.

"*The Gondoliers* has not 'caught on' in New York," bluntly wrote an *Era* correspondent a day or two later. Nor did the situation show any sign of improving in the days that followed. And because of this it wasn't long before Carte himself took a hand in it, going over to New York to rectify whatever needed rectifying in person.

Various reasons were advanced for the new opera's failure to attract, and among those reasons was the cast that had been chosen to play it. It was a cast that somehow lacked any star quality or even - very unusually for a D'Oyly Carte cast - self-confidence. Among those who particularly disappointed (which was almost all of them) was George Temple, who had been Captain Corcoran in *HMS Pinafore* when Billington made his D'Oyly Carte debut; who had been the Sir Despard who had come a cropper in Hull; and who now in *The Gondoliers* found himself cast as the Duke of Plaza-Toro.

Clearly changes were needed, and changes were quickly made. In effect Carte re-staged the whole opera; while with regard to the casting his main decision was to cable to Richard Temple, who was not in the London production, to come and take over the part of Giuseppe, and to Fred Billington to come and take over Don Alhambra.

On February 18th the new staging received its first performance. The changes undoubtedly worked – up to a point. Certainly both Richard Temple and Billington proved their worth. But despite their efforts, and even adding the original and re-staged productions together, *The Gondoliers* in New York lasted not much more than three months. *The Mikado* on its New York debut four and five years previously, it is worth reiterating, had had a run nearly three times as long.

Billington as Don Alhambra, with Leonore Snyder as Gianetta and Mary
Duggan as Tessa, New York, 1890
(Collection: David Stone)

65

Back again in Britain, Billington settled once more into the routine of provincial touring. But now in one respect the touring programme took on something of a difference. With the launching of *The Gondoliers*, Richard D'Oyly Carte had no fewer than ten full-length G&S operas to choose from when it came to deciding on the repertoire for each of his touring companies. And in the case of "C" Company, the Company in which Billington spent most of the decade that followed, he expanded the repertoire on virtually an annual basis.

Thus in 1891 "C" Company toured *The Mikado*, *The Yeomen of the Guard*, *The Gondoliers* and *Iolanthe*. In 1892 they added *Patience*; in 1893 *The Pirates of Penzance*; in 1894 *HMS Pinafore* and *Trial by Jury*; in 1895 *The Sorcerer*, *Princess Ida* and even *Cox and Box*. And Billington's repertoire of parts duly expanded in consequence.

During these years he now played five of Barrington's original parts: Dr Daly; the Sergeant of Police; Archibald Grosvenor (a new part for him, and a surprising switch given the impact he'd made as Colonel Calverley); King Hildebrand and Pooh-Bah. He played the two W.H. Denny parts, Wilfred Shadbolt and Don Alhambra. He played Dick Deadeye, Private Willis and the Judge in *Trial by Jury*. Now recognition was coming thick and fast:

"Mr Billington is best known and admired as the jailer in *The Yeomen*, but he makes a powerful Grand Inquisitor and sings with distinguished success."

(*Western Mail*, Cardiff, 1891)

"Private Willis, if not a very exacting role, yet requires a baritone of no mean power for a telling rendering of the opening song in the second act, 'When all night long', and here Mr Fred Billington scored, as usual, a great hit."

(*Bath Chronicle*, 1894)

"Dick Deadeye, as represented by Mr Fred Billington, was from every point of view a success."

(*Huddersfield Daily Chronicle*, 1894)

"Perfect indeed was Mr Fred Billington's personation of Dick Deadeye, one of the most humorous and finished performances of the evening."

(*Era* Edinburgh correspondent, 1895)

"Mr Fred Billington created continuous mirth and enjoyment by the stolidity of his performance as the Sergeant of the Police. Of course his famous song of the unhappiness of a constable's existence was several times encored."

(*Western Morning News*, Plymouth, 1895)

Moreover, as well as having his parts in G&S, Billington also had a part in *The Nautch Girl*, which "C" Company included in their repertoire during part of 1892. *The Nautch Girl*, the first of what would be no fewer than eleven non-G&S full-length works put on at the Savoy during the 1890s, was a comic opera with a fantasy Indian background; and Billington's part in it was that of the Rajah of Chutneypore:

"The role of the Rajah suits Mr Fred Billington so admirably that it might have been created for his special benefit. As the very blue-blooded monarch endowed with a prominent 'bump of consanguinity', and surrounded by a host of impecunious relatives for whom he contrives to find lucrative situations at Court, he is responsible for one of the most effective solos in the opera, constructed on 'The House that Jack built' principle. His rendering of it proved irresistible, and he was deservedly encored."

(*Leicester Mercury*)

And talking of the Court – though in this case the real Court rather than a comic opera substitute – the highlight of Billington's provincial tours in the 1890s was a Royal Command performance of *The Mikado* given before Queen Victoria at Balmoral Castle on September 4th 1891. In the wake of that performance, he was quoted as saying a few years later, he was "introduced to Her Majesty at her own request by Sir Henry Ponsonby [her Private Secretary]" which made it sound as though she'd picked him out to the exclusion of everyone else.

But it wasn't quite like that in reality. Here's how another member of the Balmoral cast described this part of the night's proceedings. At the end of the performance itself the Company sang the National Anthem

"and then Her Majesty retired to her private apartment, and a little later Sir Henry Ponsonby was instructed to summon the following members of the Company into the Royal presence: Mr E.H. Beresford [the Business Manager], Mr George Thorne, Mr Fred Billington, Mr Richard Clarke, Miss Rose Hervey [Nanki-Poo and Yum-Yum] and Miss Kate Forster.

To these ladies and gentlemen the Queen expressed the high gratification both their singing and acting had afforded her that evening; enquired the strength of the Company; and, on being told forty-eight by Mr Beresford, expressed her astonishment that so large a Company could possibly appear in so small a space [the castle ballroom, in which the performance had taken place]."

There are two points to note here. First that the Queen, in writing up the occasion in her Journal, gave no indication whether she considered Billington to be as fat as (or fatter than) Rutland Barrington when she'd seen the latter play Giuseppe at Windsor Castle earlier that same year – see page 20 – though Billington was one of those she picked out for praise.

The second point is that the account quoted above was written by George Thorne, who in the Balmoral performance had of course played Ko-Ko, and had duly taken centre stage in the process; and that said, it's time for him to take centre stage, albeit briefly, here too.

In 1891 George Thorne was thirty-five and had been with D'Oyly Carte ten years. As previously implied, he had first been teamed with Billington for the 1885-86 *Mikado* run in New York. And right from the start, it seems, the two of them, as Ko-Ko and Pooh-Bah, had struck up a highly effective and significant stage rapport.

Following the New York *Mikado*, their association had been put on hold while Billington was away on the first Continental tour. It had then been resumed in New York with *Ruddigore*. Now in the early 1890s it reached its height in every opera in which they appeared prominently together, a fact which any number of reviewers were quick to notice:

[*The Mikado*]
"Mr George Thorne ... was ably seconded by Mr Fred Billington."
(*Bath Chronicle*, 1893)

[*The Gondoliers*]
"It was a positively exciting pleasure to be witness last evening to the reception accorded to Mr George Thorne and Mr F. Billington."
(*Manchester Courier*, 1894)

And what that meant could be summed up like this: that just as Billington was coming firmly to establish himself as the most popular provincial equivalent of Rutland Barrington, so Thorne had become the most popular provincial equivalent of George Grossmith.

Yet how good a performer was Thorne, and how did he and Grossmith compare? Physically they were much of a kind: short, wiry and irrepressibly energetic. Both had mobile and expressive faces, Thorne's "facial contortions" as Ko-Ko, wrote one reviewer, being "the wonder of all who behold them". Vocally they were two of a kind as well.

But there was at least one real difference between them, and that had to do with acting ability. Thorne was a genuine actor in a way that Grossmith never quite became, and a "thinking" actor too. This showed most clearly in his portrayal of Jack Point in *The Yeomen of the Guard*, and particularly in his handling of that opera's ending, which he made straightforwardly tragic as against the more ambivalent, even semi-comic way in which Grossmith handled it. And so convincing did he make that ending that, before long, his lead was being followed elsewhere and would be followed, too, by every other D'Oyly Carte performer who played Jack Point thereafter – to the extent that one theatrical paper eventually pronounced – maybe tongue in cheek, maybe not – that while Grossmith had been the original Jack Point, it was George Thorne who actually "created" the part.

But even allowing for what he achieved as Point, it's possible that his best part of all was Bunthorne in *Patience*, the first G&S part he played, and an "acting" part if ever there was one. So much, on the provincial circuit, did he make the part his own that he became known – and was even advertised – in some places as "Bunthorne Thorne".

Yet while he had most things going for him in terms of talent and stagecraft, there was one ingredient needed for a totally successful career that he lacked - and that ingredient was luck. On this count the contrast between Grossmith and himself could scarcely have been more pointed; for while Grossmith was one of those people who mostly struck lucky in life, Thorne was one for whom, in three crucial ways, the luck refused to run.

First in this connection, he endured frequent bouts of ill-health. Here is another extract from that *Leicester Mercury* review of *The Nautch Girl*:

> "Unfortunately Mr Thorne is suffering from a severe affection of the throat, contracted last week at Nottingham. This necessitated the elimination of one or two of his most telling solos. Still, though he evidently appeared at no slight personal inconvenience, and contrary to the advice of his medical attendant, he kept faith with the public, and was accorded a highly flattering reception."

So, on balance, that was all right – or just about – and at least on that occasion he "appeared". But when towards the end of 1896 D'Oyly Carte included him in a Company sent to visit South Africa, he was off with illness a substantial portion of the time. Grossmith, by contrast, had had only one serious bout of illness during the whole twelve years of his D'Oyly Carte career.

Secondly where the question of ill-luck came (or at least in this respect *may* have come) into the picture, there was his married life. In 1883, while touring *Patience*, he had married another member of the Company, Geraldine Thompson. It had all been very romantic. The two of them had simply disappeared one Saturday morning without telling anyone else what they were going to do, and had come back, the knot happily tied, an hour or two later. But in due course their marriage got into difficulties; and at some point, it seems, the two of them separated. Grossmith, by contrast, made a supremely happy marriage.

And third – the way in which luck ran against Thorne most obviously of all – he was never chosen to perform in Central London; never, that is, beyond those two Savoy matinees of *Ruddigore* given by the America-bound Company, and they hardly counted. Not once did he get the nod, not even in the years after 1889 when Grossmith was no longer in D'Oyly Carte, and there were parts galore being handed out in the many productions put on at the Savoy during those years.

Which takes us conveniently back to Fred Billington. Because while the chance to be involved in a lengthy run at the Savoy never came Thorne's way, the same was not true of Billington. For in the summer of 1896 Billington received a call to come and play Pooh-Bah in a revival at that theatre of *The Mikado*.

"Yours sincerely, Helen D'Oyly Carte", 1896-1900

"On Wednesday, in consequence of the indisposition of Mr Fred Billington and Miss Jessie Bond, the parts of Pooh-Bah and Pitti-Sing were played by Mr Jones Hewson and Miss Bessie Bonsall respectively."

(Era, January 16th 1897)

It was a call that could fairly be described as unexpected.

By the summer of 1896 it might have seemed *The Mikado* had been going for ever, though in fact it was still only just over eleven years old. Yet already it had had one London/Savoy revival. And now it was having a second – a further indication of its special popularity, considering that up to that time only three of the other full-length G&S operas had even had a first one.

This second *Mikado* revival had opened the previous November. It had, admittedly, been withdrawn at the beginning of March to accommodate the opening of what was to prove the final G&S collaboration, *The Grand Duke*. But as all G&S aficionados know, *The Grand Duke* never really established itself, and on July 11th *The Mikado* was brought back to re-take its place in turn.

In this revival as, indeed, in the previous one, the role of Pooh-Bah was being played by its creator, Rutland Barrington. Barrington had also played the leading role in *The Grand Duke*, and with the return of *The Mikado* he quickly decided he'd had his fill of Japanese Gilbert and Sullivan:

"I did not look forward with any special pleasure to my reappearance as Pooh-Bah" (he wrote in his autobiography) "as I had got rather tired of the part during the long original run; and my forebodings were realised, as after playing it [again] I began to feel as if I had never played anything else, and it so worked on my brain that I felt compelled to ask Carte to release me …"

It was the urgent need to find a replacement for Barrington that led Carte to call for Billington.

But if it was a call that was unexpected, it was also one that, given the tight timescale, was eminently sensible. Billington had been playing Pooh-Bah on and off ever since that first performance in Brighton before the 1885-86 American trip, and rather more on than off – a total around fifteen hundred times already. Consequently he knew the part by heart. He knew it backwards. No less crucially, he had always consciously played it on the lines dictated by Gilbert and Sullivan themselves, so he needed no extra instruction on how to put it across. His first performance of the part at the Savoy was given on Monday July 20th, Barrington having given his final performance of the run two days before.

Barrington and Billington – Billington and Barrington – they were similar, if not near identical, in so many ways. Their very names emphasised this: both beginning with "B" and ending in "ington". They played – or had played – or would play – most of the same parts. They were more or less the same age, their births being separated by no more than eighteen months. They were both tall (Barrington was over six foot) and of similar build. They both, all their lives - as I've suggested before and if I'm right - had a middle-aged feel about them. How, then, can they be differentiated? There are three points that may usefully be made by way of answer.

The first point had to do with their respective singing voices. Barrington's singing voice was variable, to say the least – see page 20 So far as is known, he had no serious vocal training. He was, first and foremost, an actor – an actor, admittedly, who was not shy about singing, who indeed regarded himself as an actor-singer; but who would never have gone far on the strength of his singing voice alone.

Billington by contrast was a vocalist of genuine accomplishment. Thanks to his long apprenticeship in church and choral music, he had received the training that Barrington lacked, and without question had benefited from it hugely. Reviewer after reviewer commented on Billington's prowess as a singer; see, as examples, the notices quoted on pages 59 and 66. As a singer he was never a prima donna, a vocalist who was determined to draw attention to himself to the detriment, if necessary, of everyone else who happened to be singing with him. But there's no doubt that in any singing contest between Barrington and himself, he (Billington) would have won hands down.

The second factor that differentiated them had to do with their respective origins and background. Barrington was the son of a would-be clergyman and a Londoner. Billington, as described earlier in this book, was the son of a wool worker and a Yorkshireman. Even if they'd not been reasonably similar in height and build they would have *sounded* different – or at any rate sounded different offstage – not just in terms of accent but to some extent of vocabulary too. Still more significant, Billington had none of Barrington's conceit. Billington might happily describe himself as "just a plain Yorkshireman". It's impossible to imagine Barrington describing himself, even in fun, as "just a plain Londoner".

In the same way it seems not unlikely that, for all his stolid presence on stage, Barrington, the Londoner, lived life at a faster pace than Billington the provincial. And though it's obviously possible to make too much of this, it's not totally fanciful to think of the two of them as the hare and the tortoise – that is, with Barrington as the hare always keen to get on with things, and Billington as the tortoise more comfortable taking his time. Was it entirely chance that, when it came to G&S, Barrington became a star on his first appearance, while Billington had several years in the operas before his own star qualities became fully developed? Was it entirely chance that Barrington now felt he needed a change of professional focus – a need to get away from G&S – while Billington was content to remain as he was and to play the same roles in the same set of operas for as long as his performing career lasted?

Which brings us back to Pooh-Bah and Billington at the Savoy. Because he took over some way into *The Mikado's* run, Billington missed out on the reviews which the opera's revival had initially spawned. But there was another occasion which specifically drew certain reviewers to the theatre, and that was the Japanese opera's official thousandth Savoy performance on October 31st; and thanks to this, the omission was to some extent rectified. "Mr Fred Billington," wrote the *Era* reviewer of this performance,

> "had the unenviable task of following Mr Rutland Barrington in the role of Pooh-Bah, a part that he played with considerable intelligence, though with scarcely sufficient lightness of touch."

Given that up to this time Barrington had been the only person to have played the part at the Savoy except for occasional appearances by understudies, it was inevitable that comparisons should be made between himself and his successor, whoever that successor had happened to be.

Nor was it only press reviewers who made the comparison. So, naturally enough, did ordinary members of the theatre-going public. "Billington is not equal to Barrington as Pooh-Bah, but he is very amusing," wrote William Winckworth, a music student, in his diary, after seeing him in the part one day in October.

In all, Billington was to play Pooh-Bah at the Savoy for seven months, less a fortnight towards the end of the year when he was temporarily drafted back into the touring company. Then in February of the new year, 1897, *The Mikado* was withdrawn in favour of a new Savoy production, a non-Gilbert, non-

Sullivan comic opera called *His Majesty*. And Billington, having by then come to be regarded, almost despite himself, as a recognised member of the Savoy Company, was cast to play a part in that too. Coming after Pooh-Bah, though – coming, even more, after *The Mikado* as a whole – it was not a happy exchange.

For *His Majesty* was, quite simply, a piece with little to commend it. It had a convoluted plot. It had music that was mostly too heavy and earnest for comic opera. It had an uninspiring Ruritanian setting. And it had characters that, taken overall, lacked any real humour, life or sparkle.

The lead character was a King Ferdinand, the "His Majesty" of the title, a part given, as with the lead character in most of G&S, to the Company's light comedian. And in the event no fewer than three of the most famous D'Oyly Carte light comedians were to play it during its run: George Grossmith, C.H. Workman (of whom more anon) and Henry Lytton (ditto) – though of the three only Lytton played it for more than a handful of performances.

Billington's part was that of another king, King Mopolio; and as with King Hildebrand when contrasted with King Gama in *Princess Ida*, it was a part that came off a fairly unrewarding second best:

> "Mr Fred Billington was appropriately ponderous as the King of Osturia."
>
> (*The Times*)

> "Mr Fred Billington as the ridiculous King Mopolio – a most interesting part – does all he can [with it] – he can [do] no more."
>
> (*Illustrated London News*)

Or that's what got printed. It seems much more likely that the word "interesting" was either intended ironically or was a misprint.

His Majesty, it can be stated without hesitation, was not a success. It was unconvincing in its original form, and only partly less so when, after a month, it was somewhat revised. It struggled along for nine weeks in all (February 20th – April 24th) when it was withdrawn in turn, and had its place taken by another G&S revival, in this case *The Yeomen of the Guard*.

By then, however, Billington was no longer on the Savoy cast list. Towards the end of March he had been taken ill – and as it turned out, quite *seriously* ill. It was the first time in his D'Oyly Carte career that he'd gone down with an illness or other physical affliction that hadn't cleared up within at most a few days. Occasionally he'd had the odd performance or performances off with minor ailments of one sort or another. Yet the total number of his absences had been no more than might have been the case with any long-serving performer; and it may even be that staying, as he mostly did, in hotels had kept his health on a more even keel than it would have been had he been obliged to endure the varied discomforts of an endless series of theatrical digs.

Billington (right) and Walter Passmore in *His Majesty*. (*Illustrated London News)*
(Photograph: Peter Brading)

But this time his illness was something more debilitating. This time it wasn't just a case of his missing the odd performance. Not only did he not come back for the final rites of *His Majesty*, but – as the *Era* eventually explained:

> "Mr Fred Billington, who was to have played Wilfred Shadbolt in the forthcoming revival of *The Yeomen of the Guard* ... will be unable to do so, as owing to severe indisposition he has been ordered by his doctor to take a complete rest for three months."

What that "severe indisposition" actually was can now only be guessed at. Some years later he himself described it as "a severe nervous illness", which may provide a clue but which equally could mean anything. It seems a fair bet, though, that it had been brought on by his excess weight – now nineteen stone, if not more – and general sedentary lifestyle. For the doctor, having ordered him to take a rest, also (it seems) ordered him to start taking regular exercise.

Regular exercise. Meaning, perhaps, doing some walking? If that was the case, Billington was having none of it. "Walking," he was once contemptuously quoted as saying. "Walking for walking's sake is terrible rot!" And instead, apparently for the first time in his life, and with or without prompting, he tried his hand at golf.

The result was astonishing. For almost immediately he got the golfing bug. Almost immediately the game hooked him. Almost immediately he became a golf obsessive, a golf fanatic. And, perhaps even more astonishingly, he became a golfing ace, able to challenge, and at times beat, the best.

> "Since I started I have played them all – Vardon, Herd and others – and beat them for quids. I have £3 of Sandy Herd's yet."

This is difficult – as difficult in its way as trying, as a southerner, to do justice to the life and personality of a thoroughbred Yorkshireman. As a confirmed walker myself, I totally disagree with Billington's dismissal of walking as "rot". As for golf, well, to quote just one sentence on the subject in a newspaper article I read recently –

> "If a round of golf takes four hours ... the actual time when someone is hitting a ball is approximately three minutes"

and what more needs to be said than that?

Still there it is. And in the case of Billington, golf not only became his passion but the subject of any number of his "stories". I began the first chapter of this book with one of those stories, the "Clergyman and Buttons!" story, which was undoubtedly his favourite. Here now is another:

> "I was asking [a professional] the other day why, after making one round of seventy-three he should have fallen off so. He explained some trouble he had at about the eighth hole, and said that after this he had no more chance than a snowball in hell.

I like that expression 'a snowball in hell'. It's new to me."

Which is not the most obvious punchline for a golfing story. But you can't have everything.

The three months he'd been ordered to rest passed. At the beginning of August he was back on stage again, fully recovered.

But not on stage at the Savoy. Not on stage in his unloved Central London. As it turned out, his time at the Savoy was no more than a passing break in the normal routine of his career – that is, touring the provinces. Even so, it was not an insignificant time in terms of his D'Oyly Carte position and status as a whole. For, if nothing else, it underlined the fact that as a G&S performer he had genuinely come of age. No longer was he, as he'd previously been, just one of many performers on the D'Oyly Carte books. Rather he'd become an unquestioned star, and a star whose face, not to mention figure, was recognised all over the provinces, and whose popularity had become such that, as it was later put:

> "Without the name of Fred Billington on the bills no D'Oyly Carte touring Company could be considered fully complete and welcome anywhere."

And this was a considerable - if not unique - achievement. To most British actors and singers who are or have been stars, the provinces are at best a secondary world. What counts and counted for *them*, what gives and gave them their fame, is and was appearing in Central London. But Billington turned that aphorism on its head. For him it was London that was the secondary world. For him it was the provinces that counted. For him it was touring the provinces that was the backdrop to stardom and fame.

The sense that he had now achieved stardom comes through in three ways. First in the glowing notices he was now receiving more often than not. Second in his pay, which by this time was £20 a week. Only a few others in the touring companies at the time received even half that amount. And third, he was now being asked by various newspapers to give interviews.

How many interviews he eventually gave in all, and which newspaper actually landed the first of them, are questions that are easier to ask than to answer. But a possible candidate for the first interview was one published in the *Midland Counties Express* in Wolverhampton on December 12th 1896. The journalist who conducted that interview opened his account of it as follows:

> "The announcement that each evening during the present week Mr Fred Billington would appear at the Grand Theatre, Wolverhampton led me to seek out that talented actor, and I had a very happy half hour's chat with the great Yorkshireman on Monday afternoon."

And there is no doubt that "the great Yorkshireman" revelled in the interview himself, and was quite prepared to do as much talking as was required of him:

"I have been with D'Oyly Carte" (he said, in answer to one of the journalist's questions) "a matter of eighteen years, being only seven weeks out during that period, and there may be justification for saying that no other actor has spoken more of Gilbert and Sullivan's words or sung more of their music than myself."

Less than two years later, in September 1898, the Blackpool *Gazette and News* followed Wolverhampton's lead with an interview headed

"Pooh-Bah: a chat with Fred Billington"

and the interviewer in this case began by informing his readers that "there are few better known names in the annals of comic operas than Mr Fred Billington" – going on to state that "after twenty years in the D'Oyly Carte Companies Mr Billington is as mirthful and tuneful as ever and bids fair to [continue] long after the bones of the nineteenth century have been flattened out of recognition …."

Was this intimation that he intended to continue doing what he was doing in any way surprising? Hardly. He may have loathed "work". But playing in G&S, as he told another interviewer a few years later, wasn't work in the sense he thought of work at all. Rather, it was a pleasure. He was simply doing something he enjoyed; doing it, too, in places where he felt thoroughly at home – that is, in the cities and towns of the provinces. That part of the pleasure was crucial; and on another later occasion he explained what it was about the provincial round and provincial audiences that he so relished:

"Provincial audiences are variable in every way. This makes touring interesting. We never know what to expect. Fresh audiences, fresh orchestras, towns, theatres, dressing rooms, lodgings and hotels all offer such constant variety that there is no likelihood of getting stale, as one is prone to become after a long run in London …"

Or, as he put it to the Wolverhampton interviewer, touring was preferable to London "because you get fresh audiences every week, you are kept bright and up to the mark and it makes you 'buck up'." And, later again, he expanded on the theme of the different audiences he'd encountered and the differing degrees of their appreciation of G&S. The best G&S audiences of all, he claimed, were in the Scottish towns and the Northern English towns:

"In Edinburgh, Aberdeen, Glasgow and Newcastle the strongest evidence of appreciation is shown. In the Midlands, also, the operas meet with loyal support. But I must not forget our good Irish friends and patrons, who always give us such [a] warm welcome that we look forward to our periodical visits to Dublin and Belfast with infinite pleasure.

[However] Yorkshire, my native county, I cannot speak so well of, except perhaps Sheffield. Sheffield, by the way, was the very first town to understand Gilbert's humour."

What can one say about that last assertion except "Pass the mustard"? It should also, surely, be taken with a pinch of salt. Was he really correct in suggesting that Yorkshire audiences were less enthusiastic about G&S than other audiences in the North and elsewhere? It seems somewhat doubtful.

One thing that does emerge, though, is that certain of his less than totally eulogistic notices emanated from Yorkshire sources, including the following couple from his long abandoned home town:

"Mr F. Billington acted with good taste the character of Pooh-Bah, though his 'make up' hardly came up to previous representation."
(*Huddersfield Daily Chronicle*, 1888)

"Of the gentlemen Mr Fred Billington made a popular reappearance in the character of Wilfred Shadbolt, and though his portrayal of the part was perhaps a trifle more good-natured than the author intended, yet Mr Billington was throughout a thoroughly capable exponent, his singing being an especially notable feature in his performance."
(*Huddersfield Daily Chronicle*, 1899)

Then there was Hull:

"The performance of *The Gondoliers* last night in the Grand Theatre was so good that it ought to have been better.

It would have been better had it not seemed as though the performers regarded it as their chief aim in life to 'romp' through it …

Mr Fred Billington was a sinner in this respect. His conception of the part he played is funny and undoubtedly popular. But the *Mail* musical critic present last night holds that it is wrong. Instead of a dignified Don Alhambra Mr Billington gives us a jovial Friar Tuck."
(*Daily Mail*, Hull, 1900)

As before his Savoy interlude, Billington was playing a part in every G&S opera then in the repertoire – which is to say, the complete canon from *Trial by Jury* to *The Gondoliers*, with the single exception of *Ruddigore*, in which he was never to play again. He also for a year or two played in *Utopia Limited*, the last but one G&S collaboration, taking the Barrington part of King Paramount. It may even be that in 1901 he played a few times in the Sullivan/Basil Hood opera, *The Rose of Persia*. The only G&S/D'Oyly Carte opera in which he never played was *The Grand Duke*. The Company in which he appeared throughout these years was once again "C" Company which, because it now performed so many of the operas, had eventually been re-named D'Oyly Carte's "Repertoire" Company.

For all that Billington was now back in the provinces, though, there was one sense in which he still kept up a London connection in a highly significant way. It was all to do with his continuing friendship with Helen Lenoir, the unlikely friendship that had begun during his early weeks in the capital back in 1879.

Helen Lenoir was by this time Mrs D'Oyly Carte, having married Richard D'Oyly Carte as his second wife in 1888. And if she had been all but indispensable to the running of his affairs in the late 1870s and the 1880s, she was now indispensable with a capital "I" and with the "all but" prefix long removed.

The reason for this could be summed up in three words: ageing and illness. None of the "triumvirate", Carte, Gilbert and Sullivan, were getting any younger, and during the 1890s all three suffered long bouts of illness, with the loss of energy and drive this inevitably entailed. Of the three, Gilbert's bouts were the least severe, or at any rate the least life-threatening, but it was the decline in *Carte's* health that had the most far-reaching effects.

For even if Gilbert and Sullivan, the creative artists, wrote no more works for the stage – or indeed no more works full stop - life for everyone else would still go on. They could work as and when they felt up to it; whereas Carte, the businessman, had a theatre to keep running and touring companies to keep on the road – and this had to be done week in, week out whether he felt up to it or not.

And during the 1890s it was Helen, eight years his junior and still retaining much of the energy and drive that, as the decade progressed, were gradually draining from *him*, who took on what at times became the sole responsibility for doing all that, while simultaneously acting to some extent as his carer.

Where Billington was concerned it seems likely that he and she kept in touch throughout these years. It seems distinctly possible that it was she who had suggested him as Barrington's replacement as Pooh-Bah at the Savoy. But it also seems to have been the case that after his return to the provinces their friendship took on a new depth and importance; or certainly - and strikingly - did so on *her* side.

Which was a striking fact in itself. For if it was a friendship remarkable for having come into being in the first place, it was only a shade less remarkable that it should still be flourishing now. After all, the relative positions and status of the two of them in D'Oyly Carte hadn't changed in the interim. Helen was still, to an even more obvious extent than before, his employer and part of the D'Oyly Carte management. Billington was still, exactly as before, no more than one of her employees. Employer and employee: were they not regarded in Victorian times as two different species? – two different species who, whatever the field of employment, both knew their places in life and rarely ventured into each other's worlds?

Yet here was Helen wearing her employer's hat and finding no difficulty in breaking the strictest of unwritten rules and treating Billington as a fully-fledged equal.

So what was it – what was the particular set of circumstances – that made his friendship so valuable to her at this juncture? The answer lay in the endless weight of responsibility she was carrying on her shoulders virtually the whole time.

She needed a confidant, someone with whom she could share her problems, her difficulties; someone to whom she could unburden herself, to whom she could pour out her irritations and frustrations; someone she could use as a sounding board for plans and ideas; someone who, along with all that, was discreet. During the run-up to *His Majesty* she had to some extent cast George Grossmith in this role. But with Billington she took things much further.

For somehow the chemistry between them worked so well that Billington filled the role with a helpfulness and sense of awareness that was impressive in a man who was a confirmed bachelor. "I am not married; I never have been and never will be," he told an interviewer in 1906. As a confirmed bachelor, he was a man who might be thought to have had little understanding of women. As a man who lived permanently on the move and had no real responsibilities of his own, he might be thought to have had little understanding of the problems besetting someone with responsibilities that could seem endless. And yet, somehow, the necessary understanding was there.

Furthermore it wasn't a case of the two of them simply getting together at times for a chat. Rather, because she was permanently based in London while he, week after week, was somewhere miles away on tour, nearly all their communicating was done by letter.

How many letters passed between them altogether is impossible to say, for the vast majority of them have not survived. Apart from a single one dated June 1897 that is as near as makes no difference illegible, all that remain are copies of letters she wrote to him between late December 1899 and the beginning of February 1900, plus a further one the following May. But there are enough of them – fourteen of them covering this short period alone – to leave no doubt about the value she placed on his friendship and the way, even, that she depended on it; and for this reason it's worth reproducing a number of them in large part or actually in full.

The first of them was dated December 22nd, and referred with anxious concern to her husband's state of health. The "Repertoire" Touring Company, then playing at Eastbourne, was due to play next at Folkestone:

"Dear Mr Billington

Many thanks for sending your Folkestone address. I do not know yet if we shall get down there. It depends on the weather and partly also whether rooms are to be got. I think it possible Mr Carte would like to go there next week if he could get proper rooms, but in his case there are so many difficulties as to their being properly warmed and on the same level and not where there are any draughts, so it makes it rather risky going about in this cold weather, and the doctor is rather nervous about it. If you are at the Queen's [Hotel] you might let me know how the rooms there are, and whether they are fearfully full. Also at the Pavilion, which is where we always used to go.

I shall be delighted to have your letter about the Company.
Yours sincerely
Helen D'Oyly Carte."

Her second letter – in this instance no more than a note – followed the next day, December 23rd:

"Dear Mr Billington
The biscuits from Edinburgh have just arrived. Sincere thanks."

Shortbread as a Christmas present, perhaps?

And her third letter was written just four days after that. Health concerns were her subject once more, and health concerns not only relating to Carte:

"Dear Mr Billington
I am very sorry to find you are still ill. I should think the only course is for you to go straight to Hastings [the Company's next date] if you are quite clear you will not be able to play at Folkestone; no doubt it is a milder place. Anyway let me know what is settled, because as things are and as the weather has got still colder, I think it is almost impossible that the doctor would let Mr Carte go to Folkestone. It is much more likely he might let him go to Hastings.

I will certainly enclose the cheque for £20. Mr Gridley ought naturally to give you that under such circumstances at any time if you ask him for it, and the only reason I can conceive is that he may be short of money, business having been perfectly awful during the last two weeks. I daresay he does not like to send up for more than he can help."

"Mr Gridley" was Lawrence Gridley, a one-time player of the Pooh-Bah parts himself. Now he was the Repertoire Company's Business Manager (sometimes called "Acting" Manager) responsible for paying its members their weekly salaries. It seems clear from a number of letters she wrote at this time that Helen was not terribly impressed with him in his managerial capacity, including this one to Billington dated December 30th:

"Dear Mr Billington
Many thanks for writing me about the [play] bills. The whole question seems to be whether it is the custom at Hastings to put up the new bills on Friday or on Saturday, and I think you will discover this by seeing at the end of the visit whether they cover up ours before the Saturday. If they do we shall have a legitimate cause of complaint, and you may be quite sure I will deal with it. I will in writing to Mr Gridley mention to him that our bills were not out by Friday night, and tell him to ascertain what they do and watch this. It is also his business to do this. I am afraid he is not very [*illegible*] about it."

"Mr Gridley" was again the main subject of her next letter to Billington, a letter written on January 4th in the new year. This time she'd got as far as weighing up the pros and cons of replacing him, partly on the strength of some less than satisfactory travel arrangements he had recently made:

"Dear Mr Billington

About the acting management, I consider it is a very serious matter. Of course when an acting manager seems to have absolutely no idea of arranging railway journeys comfortably and no power over the railway people, it often means illness for the Company as has happened two winters running, and I do not think we can go on with it, but we don't want to jump from the frying pan into the fire …

It is very difficult to get a really good man. Mr Redford [Robert Redford, another of the touring business managers] wrote us suggesting his brother a little while ago who was at Hull, and if you know him you could tell me privately all about him. What puzzled me was that I understand Mr Le Breton [Henry Le Breton, Manager for a few months of Carte's "D" Company] has taken his place, and Le Breton was not by any means up to the work of our companies, so I can hardly understand how Mr Redford's brother would be, but of course there may be some private reason for his going that I do not know of.

Anyway if you will give this matter your attention, and find out anything you can or make us any other suggestions, I shall be only too pleased. Travelling about as you do, you are infinitely more likely to see who are the good working acting managers than I am, and very likely you may come across someone."

This flood of words – and I've by no means quoted the whole lot – could hardly emphasise better the intimate nature of the whole Helen-Billington correspondence. It's worth stressing again: these were letters written by an employer to one of her employees, asking him privately for his opinion of other employees on her books, along with yet others whom she might employ in the future. And if all that was pretty revealing, even more so was the paragraph with which she ended the same missive:

"I have just had a letter from George Thorne, a most unexpected thing. I will perhaps enclose it for you to read, as I should like to know whether it could possibly be a fact that he has been playing every day all this time. It seems to me impossible. I daresay you have heard something about him in travelling. From his letter he seems to be back again with his wife."

Thorne was no longer in D'Oyly Carte, having left the Company the previous year. Even so, he might not have been too happy if he'd known that a private letter he'd written to Helen Carte was possibly going to be shown without his permission to someone else, even if that someone else was a former colleague with whom he'd formed an excellent rapport.

Thorne and his problems, however, did not delay Helen long. For when, the very next day, she was writing to Billington again, she didn't even mention him. Instead it was seaside visits and fresh air concerns once more:

"Dear Mr Billington

Probably by the time you get this we shall have decided whether we are able to come to Hastings or not, or whether it will have to be Bournemouth. I have just wired Mr Gridley to ask for the order of the operas at Bournemouth as this may bear on it, but have no reply. The fact is as you wrote me that the only nights it would be much use coming next week would be Thursday and Friday. We had thought of coming tomorrow (Saturday) as the doctor is anxious now that Mr Carte should have a little fresh air, but I see it is *Patience* Saturday night and *Mikado* Monday and Tuesday, and neither of these are the pieces one really wants to see"

(which was an interesting comment, to say the least)

"So it is rather a question whether we should postpone till the middle of the week or whether we should make it Bournemouth. In the latter case Mr Carte might go somewhere else for this Sunday just to get some fresh air, and then come to Bournemouth later, but it all depends on some very important business which we have been working at all the week, and which comes rather to a head today, and it is not till knowing about this we can absolutely tell whether we can best get away tomorrow or later. I just write you this so that you may know we are thinking seriously of the matter and have it in hand, and of course if we decide to come I should telephone to the Hotel Manager as you suggested."

And the fact that Billington was suggesting something as obvious – to someone in her position – as this, and that his suggestion was gratefully acknowledged, suggests in turn something of the stress she was under, and emphasises once more how much she was depending on him for comfort and reassurance.

Twelve days later (January 17th):

"Dear Mr Billington

Many thanks for your further letter. Judging partly from what you wrote before, we practically decided not to trouble you about Bournemouth, and in any case as things have shaped out, we should not, I see, have got there because the legal and other matters which I had hoped might be finished off last week have dragged on (as such things usually do) and I doubt if they will be finished before the end of next week.

We cannot get on very fast with anything of that kind because of Mr Carte's health, as he has been very far from well, and the amount of time in the day when he can be allowed to work is very short. That makes everything take longer than it would otherwise."

Her next (surviving) letter was not written till February 1st, by which time her concern had moved on, at least temporarily, from Carte's health to financial matters and the general running of an opera company, and was actually, not before time, marked "Private":

"Dear Mr Billington

About [the Company's New Year season in] Hastings, I was looking at the receipts, which I had not seen before, and I noticed that they would be very fairly good for the smaller Company. But for the Repertoire Company they meant a loss; that is to say, there was a pound or two to the good on the 'current' each week. But as of course the current does not include any printing, or fees, or costumes, or anything of that sort, it means that the receipts were a loss for a Company the size of the Repertoire. Still it is not a bad place to fill up with in the winter for a fortnight, and I should think it is healthy for the people, which is a consideration."

If the last sentence of that letter was rather more upbeat than the sentences which had preceded it, the opening paragraph of the next one, five days later and once again marked "Private", was more upbeat still:

"Dear Mr Billington

About Hastings, I was delighted and thankful you should write me anything in your mind, and as a matter of fact you were perfectly right as to its being much the best business of the smaller places that we took at Christmas. It was a great deal better than Torquay, Folkestone, Eastbourne etc. The whole truth is that the Hastings theatre at the usual prices does not, [even] if crammed, hold enough for a big town Company, though it is excellent for a smaller one, but at any rate it is a nice place to fill up in during pantomime time; and if as I say, one can take current expenses and keep the Company going (especially in a nice town) it is always so much to the good."

Then it was back to getting off her chest a gripe about another member of the Company, a performer who a few years earlier had been Billington's understudy in *The Mikado* and *His Majesty* at the Savoy:

"About Mr Jones Hewson, I thought he would certainly be going to Cardiff [where the Repertoire Company had just started a two week season] but he has suddenly changed his mind and says that if we cannot put him in town [that is, at the Savoy] he would rather go to America and see his wife and come back in June.

I have told him I had much rather he went on tour till we have an opera [ready], but he seems to have an idea it would not be good for his lungs travelling about, and of course I would not like the responsibility of recommending him to do anything that was not right for his health. He might change his mind again, but I thought I would let you know how it stood up to now."

84

Why did Helen value her correspondence with Billington so much? Perhaps the underlying factor, the most important reason of all, was the knowledge that, as a man with no personal ties of his own and a readiness to go anywhere in the service of D'Oyly Carte, he never presented her with problems like that.

It might be assumed from all the above that Helen was mostly writing letters to Billington rather than anyone else during these weeks, but such was far from being the case. She sometimes gave the impression she spent her days writing letters to just about everybody, to the exclusion of everything else. In an interview a few years later Billington gave an appealing glimpse into how she operated, with particular reference to one of his favourite subjects – hotels:

> "Mrs Carte is the kind of lady who will at the same time, so to speak, be dictating a letter from London to her hotel in Rome, dictating another about the Savoy Hotel or Savoy Theatre, and dictating another to a lady in the chorus who wants a pink riband instead of a blue."

And he also paid her what, to a businesswoman, could hardly have been a more flattering compliment:

> "In my opinion she has more brain than any two men I have ever met in my lifetime. She practically runs the Savoy Hotel, Claridge's Hotel, the Berkeley, and the Grand Hotel in Rome. Nearly all the decorations in the hundreds of rooms have been suggested by her.
> A marvellous woman!"

Among the collection of surviving letters to Billington from Helen there is also one – just one – letter to Billington from D'Oyly Carte himself. Billington had asked Helen for the dates of the Company's annual vacation that year, and this was Carte's reply. It was a communication that makes very sad reading:

> "Dear Mr Billington
> Many thanks for your letter. I think we will now send down a clear notice as to the vacation, as that will probably save everybody trouble.
> About seeing you when in London, of course I shall hope this time to be able to do so, but the morning is not my good time. In fact I can never get any time then – the afternoon is more like it. But we'll arrange it somehow.
>   Yours sincerely
>   R. D'Oyly Carte."

That letter was dated May 16th 1900. A year later he – Richard D'Oyly Carte – was dead.

The Lure of South Africa, 1901-06

"One of those ladies who know nothing about theatres but who, like many people, talk a lot and blush a lot about the suppositious doings of theatrical folk, once asked me: 'Do the ladies and gentlemen always dress together?'

I replied: 'Not always'."

(Fred Billington, 1906)

The death of Richard D'Oyly Carte was – how could it have been otherwise? – a significant event in D'Oyly Carte history. It meant, for the first time, a change at the Company's very top. And this in turn meant that, after what had in effect been several years of joint management, Helen D'Oyly Carte was now indisputably in charge in her own right.

To start with, though, the change seemed to make little difference to the Company's operations. But for financial reasons, even if no other, two major changes were in the offing. The more crucial of these changes had to do with Central London. In May 1903 Helen ended operations at the Savoy, thereby bringing to a close the virtually nonstop run of D'Oyly Carte productions presented in Central London for more than twenty-five years.

Which was sad; though it was something that was almost certainly bound to have happened sooner or later. The same, moreover, could be said of the other change, which had to do with the touring companies. By the end of the 1890s the number of D'Oyly Carte touring companies had been reduced to three. From 1904 Helen reduced them to a single one.

Neither of these changes personally affected Fred Billington, now very much the senior and best known performer in the ranks. With the departure of George Thorne he was, so to speak, out on his own. Now he was not just unofficially, but officially too, the star of the Company, even if the word "star" itself was never used. Not only had his name become one to conjure with in every part of the country, but from around the turn of the century it was printed first on all the Company's public cast listings in a way that made his primacy clear (see the example on page 102).

Partly, perhaps, to balance things a little, and also to reflect the fact that he wasn't getting any younger, a couple of changes were in due course made to his workload. Having spent his previous years in the Company periodically gathering new parts, now for the first time he was asked – or asked on his own account – to drop two of them. One of those parts was the Judge in *Trial by Jury*, the other was Grosvenor in *Patience*. In addition he was no longer playing Dr Daly, though this was due to the fact that after 1900 *The Sorcerer* was dropped from the repertoire, and was to remain out of the repertoire right through the new decade and beyond. But that still left him seven parts, including his top four: Pooh-Bah, Don Alhambra, Wilfred Shadbolt and the Sergeant of Police.

The years 1901 to 1904 plus most of 1905 were fully taken up for him with the normal D'Oyly Carte provincial touring. But then, at the end of 1905, came something very different: a D'Oyly Carte tour of South Africa.

This was the third D'Oyly Carte tour of South Africa within ten years. It was not the longest of the three tours by any means, but despite this it has a strong claim to be regarded as the one that was most successful and satisfactory. The first tour (1896-97), previously mentioned in connection with George Thorne, had taken in just two venues: Johannesburg and Cape Town. The second (1902-03) had taken in seven venues. But against that it had suffered from the fact that it took place in the aftermath of the Boer War. Nor was it helped by the decision of the London management to send out what was more or less a D'Oyly Carte second team.

But this time … by this time there was no longer a second D'Oyly Carte team to send, and accordingly this time it was definitely the first team that was going. This time, too, they were to take in seven venues: Cape Town, Kimberley, Bloemfontein, Pretoria, Johannesburg, Pietermaritzburg and Durban.

They began in Cape Town on December 26th 1905; and the reviewer from the *Cape Argus* had no doubt about the impact they made:

"The warm appreciation of the crowded house which assembled last night is the best possible advertisement of the merits of the Company.

The Mikado is the piece with which the Company are opening their season. The whole thing was given with a refreshing finish and perfection of detail, resulting not merely from the merits of the individual performers, but also from continuous working together. Last night's audience went home thoroughly delighted."

The cast list on all the relevant advertising material was headed throughout the tour, as it was back in Britain, by Billington. No longer was he regarded as a second rank principal tagging along in the wake of some of the others, as had been the case with his first trips abroad in the 1880s. This time he went abroad as an unquestioned star, and this time he was duly treated like a star. The *Sunday Times* of Johannesburg, a town in which they stayed nearly two months, was especially ready to fawn on him, one of its reporters interviewing him not just once but twice – and at length – during that time. The opening paragraphs of the first interview (April 15th 1906) presented a particularly vivid picture:

"It was two p.m. and the old Savoyard was in his p-----js [*sic*] in his elegant apartment at the Carlton [Hotel], cooling down after a morning's golf and a refreshing bath.
Mr Fred Billington is a cheery Yorkshireman – he comes from Huddersfield – with snowy white locks, big brown eyes and an accent.
There is much less of Mr Billington now than there used to be. Once upon a time he could bring down the scale at a trifle over nineteen stone; now it requires a special effort on his part to touch eighteen.
'I could go to the North Pole without an overcoat,' he explained, 'but I can't stand the hot weather' …"

Pause. Or, rather, not much of a pause, as before long the interviewer had got him talking and reminiscing about life in G&S and D'Oyly Carte; and once embarked – as always when he started talking – there was no stopping him:

"Mr Billington went on to tell stories of his career at a speed that would paralyse any shorthand writer."

Some of those stories, along with other quotes from the two Johannesburg interviews, have found their way into other places in this book. Then because it became clear that one session wasn't nearly enough to exhaust his repertoire, the interviewer was moved to return a fortnight later for a second session, his account of which, when published, was given the possibly somewhat two-edged heading
                              "Fred Billington Talks Again"

and this time the text began positively cheekily:

" 'What, again?' Mr Fred Billington exclaimed as a *Sunday Times* man entered his rooms and sank his muddy boots comfortably deep in the Persian carpet. 'Do you really want me to continue that interview?'
'Your experience and bulk are abnormal,' said the pen-pusher with becoming meekness, 'and cannot well be bovrilised into the space of one short column.'

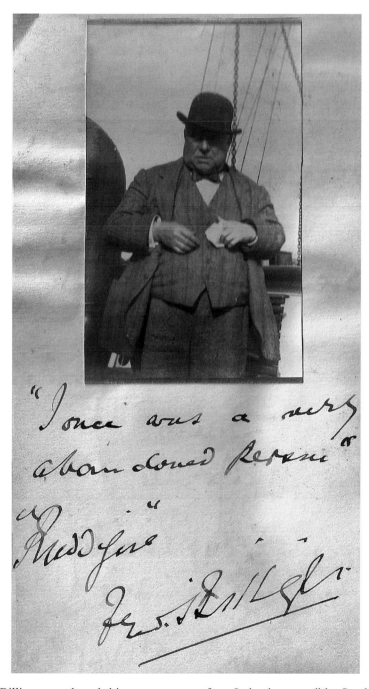

Billington on board ship, *en route* to or from Ireland or, possibly, South Africa. From an album of cast photographs
(Collection: George Low)

'Well,' answered the burly Savoyard, 'I've an idea your readers won't lose sleep if they don't read any more about me. But if you think differently, why – let her go'!"

And off her (or, rather, he) went, starting this time by talking about his early life in Yorkshire and his first weeks in London, and eventually getting on to his favourite subject of golf. And he was still in full flow when the interviewer suddenly decided he'd had enough, and in the middle of one of Billington's golf stories jumped up, desperate to get away, and "fled towards the elevator".

Billington, though, was not the only member of the Company interviewed by the paper during the Johannesburg season. There were three others who were favoured in this way. One of these was Henry Bellamy, a man potentially as interesting on the subject of D'Oyly Carte as Billington himself. Bellamy had started his Carte career as a performer, but had then gone over to the management side of things, and was Business Manager on all three of the Company's South African tours. A broad-chested, genial-looking figure with a monocle and a flamboyant moustache, he was, however, much less willing to be interviewed than Billington ever appeared to be:

"A *Sunday Times* man cornered Mr Bellamy on Thursday and asked him to talk about his career. This he declined to do until the interviewer calmly but firmly said that he would be obliged to invent a history and weave it round his photograph for publication."

Invent a history? Could any journalist have described the dubious side of his trade better? And the result in this case:

"Reluctantly, very reluctantly, he [Bellamy] then proceeded to pace his *sanctum sanctorum* and off-load a few incidents in a remarkably varied career"

after which it's only fair to say that before long he seems to have thawed completely, and was chatting away and relating a few anecdotes quite happily.

A third member of the touring Company to be interviewed by the paper was Pacie Ripple, the principal tenor. Pacie Ripple was a very odd bird, and his oddness started with his name. Unsurprisingly (?) it was not his real name, though what his real name really was is shrouded in uncertainty. This uncertainty, indeed, extends to almost every aspect of his life, starting right back with his origins.

According to an interview he gave close on thirty years later, he was born in Dublin. But that was not what he told the interviewer in Johannesburg. "Like Fred Billington," the latter informed his readers, "he is a Tyke [that is, a Yorkshireman] by birth." But unlike Billington he no longer spoke like a Yorkshireman. Twelve years he had spent in America had "knocked great chunks out of his native accent, and in their places a nice luxuriant USA twang has sprung up".

Prior to America Ripple, who had originally trained to be a civil engineer, had

> "at the age of eighteen sailed to Buenos Aires in connection with some
> big engineering contract and, to use his own words, 'I liked that job so
> well that I quit. Then I found I was suffering from what somebody has
> called a disease – I mean a tenor voice.
>   Well, he may be right. I have been cursed with one a long time now,
> but I can truthfully say it is painless and it never hurts me. And I have
> nothing to do with the woes of other people."

Still at least he showed he had a sense of humour.

As regards D'Oyly Carte, he claimed in a second later interview to have been in the Company considerably longer than was actually the case. Moreover, he hardly took to G&S in the way most D'Oyly Carte performers took to it – or at least claimed to take to it. When asked by the Johannesburg man which were his favourite operas, he said "*Iolanthe* and *Patience*". Why? Because

> "I don't like work, you see, and the tenor parts in those two plays are
> light. Consequently they are my favourites. I would rather sing Faust
> any night than Frederic in *The Pirates*. [As Frederic] you are on the
> stage all the time …"

Still if he didn't like work there was always golf. As with Billington, golf was the only form of recreational physical activity in which he indulged. Did this mean the two of them saw a fair amount of each other offstage? Possibly. But whether they did or not, Ripple freely admitted that, as a golfer, Billington was much his superior.

The fourth person interviewed by the paper – and interviewed twice, like Billington – was C.H. (Charles Herbert) Workman. And from Billington's point of view, Workman was by some distance the most important of the others.

Born at Bootle in Lancashire in 1873, he had joined D'Oyly Carte as a chorister and small part player in 1894. But he had then shot up in the ranks to such an extent that by 1898 he had become the leading touring player of the Grossmith parts. In consequence he had taken over from George Thorne as Billington's principal stage sparring partner – Ko-Ko to his Pooh-Bah, Jack Point to his Wilfred Shadbolt, and so on. And just as, on the Company's cast lists, Billington's name was being given pride of place at the top, so Workman was given a special place too – the place later given to Henry Lytton (see page 102).

"Mr Workman," wrote his Johannesburg interviewer, "is a particularly well groomed, merry-eyed, round-cheeked, mobile-mouthed, of five foot something man." And along with a well turned out appearance went modesty – modesty that at times was almost self-effacing. He was a man who, above all, liked to be liked, and in general he *was* liked.

But as a corollary to this, he was also someone who was potentially liable to be pushed around or given the brush-off by people with personalities stronger than his own; and on one occasion in 1900, for instance, he had effectively been given the brush-off by Helen D'Oyly Carte, not somebody one normally thinks of as doing that sort of thing. The brush-off came after he had requested an increase in salary. "Dear Mr Workman," she had begun a letter in response to his request,

"I see that your salary is now £8-10-0 a week, which does not seem to me at all a bad salary, especially as you have your wife also in the Company (which, as you know, is not allowed in many of the other musical companies travelling) which gives you both £10-10-0 a week. I do not think I could say anything about a further increase until … I have seen the Company …

[And since] artists, as they go on, expect salaries to increase, the only way for us when expenses get too high is to take in fresh artists at less salaries, so as to keep the Company going without its getting too expensive …"

So that put *him* in his place, as well as providing an insight into D'Oyly Carte policy and concerns at the time. And presumably she didn't send his letter on to Billington as she had previously suggested she might do with that letter of George Thorne's. Workman's wife, incidentally, was Bessel Adams, one of the choristers and small part players. Incidentally, too, Workman was another of the Company's golfers.

Despite his self-effacing character offstage, Workman as a performer was a worthy successor to Grossmith, to Grossmith's eventual London successor Walter Passmore, and to George Thorne. His association with Billington, indeed, had quickly come to be relished by D'Oyly Carte audiences to an extent almost as great as the latter's previous association with Thorne had been. In his Johannesburg interviews he talked a little about how he had first developed a taste for the stage, and he did admit to one quirkish ambition where his performance as Ko-Ko was concerned:

"Yes," (he said, presumably in answer to a question) "I do not despair of playing in the dear old *Mikado* by special Royal Command at Tokyo before the Mikado himself – in Japanese, if he wants it."

For most if not all of the South African tour he and Billington – the Lancastrian and the Yorkshireman – shared dressing rooms, and there is nothing to suggest that they didn't get on well together or that they succumbed to the traditional Lancashire-Yorkshire "Roses" rivalry. Rather there was one occasion in Johannesburg when they were firmly united against another compatriot who, it seems likely, didn't hail from either county. Here, somewhat rewritten, is an account of what happened given by Workman:

C.H. Workman as Ko-Ko
(Author's Collection)

"During the first part of the tour Billington and I were waited on in our various dressing rooms by a dresser who was engaged on our behalf in Cape Town, and who was the best and smartest dresser we'd ever had anywhere.

He was an Englishman, so we naturally trusted him, and this turned out to be a costly mistake. One 'treasury' night, at the end of a performance of *The Mikado*, we returned to our room to disrobe to find … not only that our dresser was missing, but so were our purses, watches and other valuables. It was immediately clear the two things were connected, and we both immediately erupted, Billington in what I'd call his choicest Yorkshire vernacular.

By the time we were back in our everyday clothes, though, we'd both calmed down a little, and Billington said, 'Thank the Lord, Workie, we won't have to tip him this week'."

Billington's other comment on this episode, as reported by the Johannesburg interviewer, was to the effect that "never before in my life have I given my money into the care of a dresser. I won't do it again." He also disclosed that they'd shortly afterwards found out the man was a convicted criminal.

One other member of the touring Company who must be given special mention here is the principal soubrette, Jessie Rose. As I suggested earlier, with the exception of the light comedian, the G&S soubrette is the member of the Company whose performance in three if not four of the operas most obviously affects the man playing the heavy comedian parts. Billington, talking for once of the sopranos, commented that he'd played with no fewer than thirty-six of these ladies in *HMS Pinafore* alone. But he might equally well have commented on the number of Pitti-Sings and Phoebes, as well as the Constances and two Mad Margarets, with whom he sparred at one time or another.

In a previous chapter I referred to Kate Forster and the huge impact she made as Pitti-Sing in New York.. That said, however, her association with Billington was relatively short-lived, primarily because her voice deepened to the extent that four years later she had given up playing soubrette parts and was playing contralto parts instead. It was thus as Katisha rather than Pitti-Sing that she had appeared in the performance of *The Mikado* at Balmoral.

Thereafter for several years Billington had been paired with a succession of other soubrettes, including – in *The Mikado* revival at the Savoy in 1896-97 – the renowned, opinionated and forceful Jessie Bond.

In that *Mikado* revival Jessie Bond had duly played Pitti-Sing. As with Rutland Barrington as Pooh-Bah, she had played the part in both the opera's opening run and its first Savoy revival in 1888. And given that, as previously indicated, she and Barrington had had a strong stage rapport – given that she had never played Pitti-Sing opposite (understudies apart) any other Pooh-Bah – it wouldn't have been totally surprising had she regarded Billington as a lower form of life than his predecessor.

But whether she did or not, *her* association with him lasted no longer than the seven months they played together at the Savoy, simply because at the end of *The Mikado's* run she retired from the stage and would never again play opposite *any* Pooh-Bah. Seven years later Pitti-Sing and the other Bond parts in the repertoire were being played by the second Jessie soubrette – that is, Jessie Rose.

Born sometime in the 1870s and making her D'Oyly Carte debut as a chorister in 1896, Jessie Rose was thus a product of the socially less restrictive and burgeoning feminism of the 1890s and 1900s; just as Jessie Bond, born in 1853, was unmistakably a product of rigid and straight-laced mid-Victorian respectability. A vivacious and sparky personality, she (Jessie Rose) in due course got married. And though, eventually, she and her husband divorced and she promptly married someone else, she seems to have sailed through all this without incurring any of the opprobrium she might, as a divorcee, so easily have experienced.

Her sparky – and witty - side was to be demonstrated vividly on one occasion in 1909, when she was chosen by a respected London Society called the O.P. [Old Playgoers] Club to chair one of its meetings – a meeting to which Rutland Barrington had been invited as guest speaker. Her introductory remarks are worth quoting at length:

"Ladies and Gentlemen

Your very kind reception of me tonight has made me so bold that I can no longer say, as I had meant to do, that I am nervous at finding myself in the place of honour tonight. I think the O.P. Club shows much courage in electing a chairwoman to rule on these occasions instead of a chairman, for you run a great risk every time of finding one who is at heart a suffragette, and will rule you with a rod of iron. However, like Phoebe Meryll, I love all brave men, so you are safe for tonight.

I have been asked to introduce to you that rising young actor, Mr Rutland Barrington, whose career I have watched with interest almost from the cradle – *my* cradle. And as I am as anxious as you are to hear what he has to say … I will at once give way to him, only thanking you from my heart for the wonderful kindness you have shown to such an obscure artist as myself."

Her natural *joie de vivre* was fully reflected in her performances on stage. Rutland Barrington, having eventually played opposite her, described her as a "delightful little artist". She "made a pretty and piquant Tessa," declared an *Era* critic of her performance in *The Gondoliers*, though "she might perhaps have given a more pensive note to the song 'When a merry maiden marries'." And that last comment may have had a more general significance where she was concerned. It seems likely she was at her best on stage when being unashamedly playful as the G&S soubrette is mostly required to be, rather than during those moments in certain of the operas when she has to show a genuine depth of feeling.

Having thus highlighted four of the principal performers on the South African tour, here in each case are a few examples of their tour notices. First, Billington:

[*The Pirates of Penzance*]
"Mr Fred Billington knows the part of the Sergeant of Police pretty well now. He set about creating it … in 1879 and played it for the first time that year. [As] the Sergeant last week [he] infused no end of character and fun into his role."

(*Sunday Times*, Johannesburg)

[*Iolanthe*]
"The 'fat' part of Private Willis falls [to] the lot of Mr Fred Billington, who is successful in extracting the very last ounce of fun from it."

(*Sunday Times*, Johannesburg)

[*The Yeomen of the Guard*]
"Mr Fred Billington throws plenty of character – not to mention a broad Yorkshire accent on occasion – into the part of Shadbolt … His figure does not exactly suggest the type of wooer held up as a model by modern lady novelists. He is more like the late lamented Henry the Eighth who, by the way, was of a distinctly amorous turn despite his bulk."

(*Sunday Times*, Johannesburg)

[And *Yeomen* again – this time in conjunction with Jessie Rose]
"Miss Rose … convulsed the audience by her flirtations with the enamoured head jailer (Mr Billington) as he by the dry droll manner in which he provided foil for her sallies. His facialism made an excruciatingly funny background to her mock caresses."

(The *Friend*, Bloemfontein)

Now on to C.H. Workman:

[*The Yeomen of the Guard*]
"The chief part in the piece is, of course, the jester's. Mr Workman managed it last night with an art which it would hardly be an exaggeration to call perfect. His antics, mental and physical, kept the house in a roar, the fun climaxing in the dance and song where he teaches the dull jailer his own trade.

It is but fair to indicate that the effect here achieved was owing once more to Mr Billington's collaboration in clever offset. As in farce, so in pathos, Mr Workman was seen before the play closed to be a true artist, especially in its suggestion on his features. His looks, more even than the words or the music, gave the satisfying sadness which the closing scene demanded."

(The *Friend*, Bloemfontein)

Jessie Rose as Pitti-Sing
(Author's collection)

[*Princess Ida*]
"Mr Workman was excellent as the physically and mentally misshapen monarch, King Gama. It is a great pity that he has not a great deal more to do. He was heartily encored for his singing of 'If you give me your attention ...' and was twice recalled to give 'The Disappointed grumbler' [*sic*]."

(*Cape Argus*)

[*The Mikado*: Workman as Ko-Ko]
"He is an artist to his fingertips."

(*Sunday Times*, Johannesburg)

Third, Pacie Ripple:

[*The Pirates of Penzance*]
"Mr Pacie Ripple ... was at the top of his vocal form in the long and exacting role of Frederic. His pure tenor voice is powerful and sympathetic and under perfect control."

(*Sunday Times*, Johannesburg)

This despite the fact that he'd gone on record as saying he'd rather have been singing Faust.

[*Patience*]
"Seldom is Mr Pacie Ripple given a chance in a humorous part, but as the Duke of Dunstable ... he was immense, and kept the house simmering with laughter"

(*Sunday Times*, Johannesburg)

and that despite the fact it was the smallest of his parts.

Finally Jessie Rose, this time on her own:

[As Melissa in *Princess Ida*]
"What Miss Jessie Rose doesn't know about love-making isn't worth knowing."

(The *Rand*, Johannesburg)

And what the Company as a whole on that tour didn't know about presenting G&S probably wasn't worth knowing either. But it was not only on stage that the South African tour was a huge success. Francois Cellier, the tour's Musical Director, who had also been on the second tour three years earlier, was quoted as saying that the two tours were among the most pleasant experiences of his life. Pacie Ripple, asked whether the altitude of Johannesburg – five thousand seven hundred feet above sea level – suited his voice, replied: "I like being high. It's easier to get the top notes."

But what of Fred Billington? Back in the 1880s and 1890 Billington had relished being in America. He had relished his tours of Germany and elsewhere in Continental Europe. So had he also relished South Africa?

On the one hand the answer seems to have been "Not altogether". The high altitudes were definitely not to his taste. "There is something about this air of yours," he had bluntly informed his Johannesburg interviewer. "Why, it feels like being up in a balloon. In Pretoria in *The Yeomen* I could not get my breath, and felt like an old rooster sitting on a fence after a fight." As already mentioned, he disliked hot weather. Nor was he exactly enamoured of the long railway journeys that had to be undertaken to get from one town to the next.

But by the time he arrived back in England – or at any rate not long after – it was a different story. "Africa," he told everyone who was interested, he "liked immensely". It might even be said he'd been bowled over by it, if "bowled over" isn't quite the phrase to use of a man of ultra-solid proportions who was normally proof against being bowled over by anything except food. "South Africa," he was also quoted as saying, was "the finest country in the world".

Curiously a belief later became current that he went to South Africa not just the once but on two or even all three of the D'Oyly Carte South African tours. The origin of that belief may have been an interview he gave to a Manchester journalist in March 1913, in which – according to the interviewer – he firmly stated he had visited South Africa "during my connection with the D'Oyly Carte operas" three times. That statement was in due course widely repeated and, it seems, was never corrected, either by himself or anyone else.

But *was* it correct? It was certainly not the case that he went there more than once with D'Oyly Carte. So did he go there on those other occasions under his own steam as a private individual? And if he did, *when* did he go? There was only one period in his life in which he was free long enough to make such visits practical, and this will be referred to in the next chapter.

Yet there's no doubt South Africa frequently occupied his thoughts in the months and years that followed his tour of the country with D'Oyly Carte. "Life there is so entirely different from what one is accustomed to at home, or in France, Germany or America," he would explain. "Not only theatrical but social and general life."

And he began playing with the idea that he might become part of that life – might actually emigrate and settle there himself sometime in the future – and the not-too-distant future at that.

"Long Past the Criticism Stage", 1906-14

" 'Laugh and grow fat' must surely be the motto of the Company. Mr
Fred Billington's jolly complaint must be infectious. He looks more like
a Smithfield farmer at Christmas than ever; and others in the Company
seem to be doing their best to follow him."

(Sheffield Daily Telegraph, April 1907)

The South African tour ended in July 1906, and for Fred Billington and most of
the others involved it was soon back once more to touring the British Isles,
which Billington himself had now been doing for the best part of the previous
twenty-seven years. And except for a spell when he was to be otherwise
engaged in 1908, he continued to tour in this way without anything changing
much for the next eight years.

By the same token, his star billing in the touring Company continued to be
reflected in press comments and notices such as the one from Sheffield quoted
above, when being described as "like a Smithfield farmer" made an interesting
alternative to being described as like Henry the Eighth or Friar Tuck. Then how
about this one from the *Bristol Times and Mirror* in 1909? "Mr Fred Billington
as King Hildebrand – well, he was Mr Fred Billington. There are few patrons of
the theatre who do not know what that means." Or this one from the *Evening
Express*, Aberdeen four years later:

"Mr Fred Billington, who could not proceed last night until his fervent admirers had exhausted themselves, still impersonates that unblushing and unprincipled pluralist Pooh-Bah, and his exposition of the mordant humour of the part is as effective as ever.

It is hardly necessary to say more. Mr Billington richly deserves the secure place he gained years ago in the favour of a public that has not been fickle in relation to him."

But the plum in this respect must be awarded to the Cardiff *Western Mail* which stated firmly in 1909 that

"Mr Fred Billington has long passed the criticism stage."

So that settled that. But can we pin down what ultimately made his performances so good, so iconic? The best answer to that question is contained in the following assessment penned by a journalist in his home town:

"Much of Mr Billington's success lay in a certain physical appropriateness to – and apparently also a mental affinity with – a particular Gilbertian type …

He sang well, had an excellent bass voice, and a technical accomplishment that befriended him in later years. His patter was itself an achievement, for with comparable slickness it possessed a musical quality that George Thorne's had not …

But the natural unction of the man it was, and neither his patter nor his voice, that won our hearts – and we loved him for it. We loved the balance of his art, the patness with which came the precise inflexion of tone needed here, the wink needed there, the riotous roll to the whited eye that threw our balance to the winds.

That gift he kept uninjured to the end … The gods loved him – and he never really grew old."

(Huddersfield Daily Examiner, 1917)

Just one comment needs, for the sake of that same balance, to be added to all this. Sometimes – not, it seems clear, in his case, though it can't have done him any harm – but sometimes in this life longevity can be its own reward.

For most of these years – the final years of the Edwardian era and the first years of George V – Billington continued to play all the parts he had played in South Africa; though he did eventually (in 1912) give up Dick Deadeye, and in 1913 Private Willis, which meant he had a night off every time the Company played *HMS Pinafore* and *Iolanthe*, to add to the nights he already had off when they played *Patience*.

An example of the cast listings from 1913, showing Billington's name topping the list.

Where his stage life as a whole was concerned, however, the most memorable happening of those years had to do with his appearances as Pooh-Bah. Or, rather, a period of his *non*-appearances as Pooh-Bah. The year was 1907, and it was the result of a decree issued by the Lord Chamberlain. Out of the blue the latter temporarily banned all performances of *The Mikado* in case they should offend a Japanese prince who was visiting Britain, and for several weeks the opera was absent from the Company's repertoire.

The entire episode was Gilbertian, a real-life absurdity, and an absurdity made still more absurd when it was claimed that selections from the opera had been played for some time by bands on Japanese warships. Whether, in the aftermath of it all, C.H. Workman still held on to his fantasy of playing the opera in Japan itself is, of course, another matter.

But meanwhile, an event far more important in terms of D'Oyly Carte history as a whole was taking place. Sometime before this, Helen D'Oyly Carte had decided the Company should make a temporary return to Central London to present a new series of G&S revivals at the Savoy. The result was something of a Company shake-up. For though she had originally intended using the touring Company for the Savoy season, she ended up engaging what was virtually a new Company for the purpose; and during that season (December 1906 to August 1907) this Company presented *The Yeomen of the Guard*, *The Gondoliers*, *Patience* and *Iolanthe*, and would almost certainly have presented *The Mikado* too but for the Lord Chamberlain's ban.

Even without *The Mikado*, though, the season proved such a success that before long Helen had arranged a second Savoy season on the same lines; and that second season duly opened in April 1908 and went on till the following March. This time no fewer than six of the operas were presented: *The Mikado* (the ban by then having long been lifted), *HMS Pinafore*, *Iolanthe*, *The Pirates of Penzance*, *The Gondoliers* and *The Yeomen of the Guard*.

But what of Billington in all this? Billington was not in any way involved in the first of those seasons, but was this quite the case with the second? For that second season Helen engaged Rutland Barrington, who had not been in D'Oyly Carte since his departure during the run of *The Mikado* in 1896. Barrington was now to play four of his former parts – Pooh-Bah, Captain Corcoran, Mountararat and the Sergeant of Police – plus the two Denny parts, Don Alhambra and Wilfred Shadbolt. And Billington? There's just an outside chance that, for that season, Helen decided to make him Barrington's understudy.

If this actually was her decision, it made in its way much sense. Of the six parts Barrington was taking on, there was only one – Mountararat – that he (Billington) had never played himself. All the others he was totally familiar with – even, most likely, Captain Corcoran which he hadn't played for years – and could have gone on in any of them at a moment's notice. Equally he could have gone on if necessary as Dick Deadeye or Private Willis.

But he didn't. Not once. Nor did he go on even once in any of Barrington's parts. Despite the length of that second Savoy season Barrington didn't miss a single show. Consequently, if he *was* his understudy Billington, during all the months it lasted, had nothing to do. So how did he fill the time? Did he hang around London – the London he so detested – during the day, then stick around the theatre before and during each performance waiting to see if he was needed that afternoon or night? It seems singularly unlikely.

Or did he not, when it came to it, ensconce himself in London and go anywhere near the Savoy at all? Was he during this time, as might otherwise be expected, taking his normal place in the touring Company instead? The answer to that, at least during the six months between the end of April and the end of October 1908, was "no", simply because during those months the operations of the touring Company were suspended, as they had not been before.

So … did he instead, for the first time in his life, take an extended holiday? Was it then that he made one of those additional trips to South Africa to which I referred in the last chapter? It's not impossible. On May 2nd a "Mr F. Billington", described as a "single male", boarded a ship in Southampton that was sailing to Cape Town. Can that "Mr F. Billington" have been *him*? To repeat, it's not impossible. Sailing in early May would certainly have given him the time to get to South Africa and back for late October, if that indeed is what he did.

The story moves on five years – to 1913. On May 5th of the latter year Helen D'Oyly Carte died. She had been ill for some time, and her death was not entirely unexpected. But for Fred Billington her passing must have been a considerable loss, and the strength of her warmth towards him was shown by the fact that she specifically mentioned him in her will.

"To my old friend Frederick Billington [read the relevant sentence, she left] twenty Savoy Hotel Limited five per cent debentures of one hundred pounds each (issue of 1893) now standing in my name."

Among other bequests she also left five of those shares to Francois Cellier, who had been a D'Oyly Carte stalwart pretty well as long as Billington himself. She left five hundred pounds to Henry Bellamy, her seasoned and experienced Business Manager. But it's worth stressing that Billington was the only member of the D'Oyly Carte Company then performing *on stage* to whom she made a bequest of any kind.

That, however, wasn't quite the end of it. Her will was dated March 11th 1910. But then, two years later, she had added a codicil in which she mentioned his name (along with four others) again:

"I also direct that as, since the date of my said will, I have made some additional payments to my old friend Frederick Billington the legacy of twenty Savoy Hotel Limited five per cent debentures of one hundred pounds each (issue of 1893) bequeathed by my said will to him shall be reduced to five of the said debentures"

which said reduction may have taken something of the edge off the said bequest. Or there again, it may not.

104

But the death of Helen and the gap this left in his life was not the only way in which Billington's story had moved on. By then he was approaching fifty-nine. He couldn't exactly be described as old, but by the standard of the day he was getting on a bit. People, he said, were nonetheless beginning to look on him as old, and a wonder for his age. How much longer did he see himself staying in D'Oyly Carte? When was he going to retire?

As far back as 1906 he was saying that he "should have retired two years ago", but hadn't done so because "Mrs Carte" had "often told him" she would like him to continue in the Company for as long as she held the G&S performing rights. In the years since then the idea of retirement had often been at the back of his mind. And by 1913 he had definitely decided – or said he had definitely decided – to go on for just two years more when his present contract would expire; that is, to retire in 1915, and on his retirement to emigrate. To emigrate to South Africa.

Was this a fantasy? Would he have actually done it when it came to the point? Who can tell? The pull of performing was still strong. It was easier to say he would retire at a date some time in the future than to say he was retiring now, whenever "now" might be. And in the event the point – that is, the point when a definite decision had to be made – never materialised.

For the following summer, the summer of 1914, the future changed irrevocably. And it changed not only for Billington but for pretty well everyone in the country.

What changed it was the outbreak of the First World War.

Mr. FRED BILLINGTON
As " King Hildebrand " in *Princess Ida.*

Billington as King Hildebrand: a drawing in a programme
(Collection: George Low)

"That bally Kaiser has got our Tour", 1914-16

"After a very restless night I found shooting going on everywhere and the sky blazing red, this being due to the many fires. The soldiers were now in the hotel, and it was fine to see them and the snipers on the roof at work. One young red-headed soldier shot two of the Sinn Feiners who were on top of the Post Office. The soldiers fired away the rebels' flag, and one of the traitors who tried to put it up again was at once shot down from this hotel."

(Henry Lytton in the *Umpire*, May 1916)

The outbreak of the First World War, though not entirely unexpected except in its timing by people in the know – the politicians, the military and elements in the press – came as a surprise to most other people, and immediately unleashed a wave of patriotic fervour. The war was seen as glamorous and exciting, as a great adventure; and it's not difficult to recognise at least part of the reason for this.

Britain had not been involved in a full-scale European war since the era of Napoleon a hundred years earlier. There had, admittedly, been any number of British wars in the meantime, but these were nearly all colonial wars fought by a small professional army hundreds of miles away. In each case life at home went on more or less undisturbed. The British public in general could glamorise war because they had no personal experience of what it was actually like.

And the First World War, when it broke out, was seen in similar terms to those other wars of the comparatively recent past. It would, that is to say, be a short war. Victory would be won quickly, and in a blaze of glory. The troops would be back home in four or five months – by Christmas. It was a war that, like all the others, would be fought abroad, even if "abroad" in this case was nothing like as far away as in most of the other cases. The civilian population at home would be largely unaffected by it; and among the civilian population would be the members of the D'Oyly Carte Opera Company, who would continue touring Gilbert and Sullivan just as they'd been doing in the years that had gone before.

On Monday August 3rd, the day before Britain entered the war, the Company began a week's season at the Lyceum Theatre, Edinburgh. The opera performed that night was *The Gondoliers*. And on the Tuesday the *Edinburgh Evening News* began its review of the performance like this:

"It has often been said of the British people that we take our pleasures sadly. May it not also be said that we take our dangers lightly?

At all events, in the midst of the war crisis, there was an almost crowded house at the Lyceum Theatre last night to welcome the D'Oyly Carte Opera Company, to laugh heartily at the humour of Gilbert, which never grows stale, and to enjoy with undiminished zest the rippling daintiness of Sullivan's music.

The Gondoliers was an excellent start for the week's programme, and taking that performance as a criterion, it can be said that seldom has the Company appeared in Edinburgh so well equipped in principals and chorus alike ..."

Do – or did – the British people really take their dangers lightly? Maybe. But the wildly intoxicated mood of the early wartime days was not sustained for long. Far from lasting only a few months the war, as hardly needs saying, was to last over four years; and far from people at home being unaffected by it, it impinged on their lives more and more as the months and years dragged on. Adapting to wartime realities meant learning to cope with all manner of inconveniences and privations, restrictions, rules and regulations, and somehow keeping going in the face of the ever-mounting casualty lists.

It's possible, nonetheless, that the members of D'Oyly Carte coped with it all as well as anyone. On the surface at least, their activities changed very little. They maintained their year round touring of the provinces and Outer London throughout the war's duration. They continued to present all the full-length G&S operas they'd presented before, even in 1916 bringing back *The Sorcerer* after a gap of sixteen years.

But what did change to a certain extent were the personnel who made up the Company. The longer the war went on, the more men who were needed to fight it, and in this respect D'Oyly Carte were no more immune from its effects than any other contemporary organisation. As a Cambridge journalist noted in November 1916 in a news item headed "The Stage and the Army":

"The D'Oyly Carte Company has cheerfully contributed of its younger manhood to the call of King and country since the start of the war.

A goodly number of the male chorus have already joined up for military service, and are playing their parts manfully on quite another stage … and one of the best known members of the present cast, I am told, will be leaving in the course of the next week or two to 'join up'."

That "best known" member of the cast was almost certainly the memorably named Leicester Tunks, for several years one of the Company's principal bass baritones, who duly joined up as expected. It definitely wasn't Fred Billington who, now in his sixties, was well past the joining up age. Rather Billington had continued for the first year or so of the war playing his customary parts in his customary robust and genial manner, as though to make clear that no war, no rules and regulations, no anything else was going to stop him; and his continuing presence was a particularly strong factor in helping to reassure audiences that the D'Oyly Carte Company was still the Company they remembered from prewar days. The reviewer of that Edinburgh performance of *The Gondoliers* in August 1914 had, in effect, made the point right at the start:

"The Grand Inquisitor and the Duke [of Plaza-Toro] were impersonated with all the old flavour and verve by Mr Fred Billington and Mr Henry A. Lytton."

This section of his review, though, was also a reminder that Billington was not the only member of the Company who represented continuity and reassurance of this sort. The same applied to Henry Lytton, a performer who had almost as lengthy a D'Oyly Carte pedigree as Billington himself.

Henry Lytton ("Harry" to his colleagues) was a phenomenon. He had previously spent years in the various Carte companies mostly playing one or more of the Grossmith parts, though without fully making those parts his own till C.H. Workman left the Company in 1909. But now he was fully established, now he was emphatically the man in possession; and thanks to all this he had now become the new "leader" of the Company, even though it was Billington who still headed the published cast lists. He was also now, like Billington, of an age when he was safe from call-up.

What can one say about Lytton that has not been said umpteen times before? Lytton – who would become the unofficial "King" of the Company in the great D'Oyly Carte days of the 1920s. Lytton – the only currently serving member of D'Oyly Carte ever to receive a knighthood. Lytton - the enthusiasm and devotion of whose fans was such that the applause they gave him inside the theatre could all but bring a performance to a halt, and who virtually mobbed him every time he showed his face *out*side it at the stage door.

Irrespective of the merits of any particular aspect of his performances, he had a star quality that outshone all his predecessors – all his successors too – and that never left him during all the years he spent in D'Oyly Carte. It was a quality based on an unfailing zest for what he was doing, a zest that, together

Henry Lytton as himself (top) and as Ko-Ko (below)
(Collection: Tony Gower)

with a spruce, dapper figure and a boyish sense of devilment that also never left him, seemed to render him ageless.

While it's impossible to be absolutely certain about these things, it seems fairly clear that he and Billington worked as well together as Billington had previously worked with Thorne and Workman. In Lytton's first volume of autobiography published in 1922 there is a five page section on Billington, as well as one other story about him in the book. Every reference Lytton made to him was made with unmistakable warmth, and this even applied when he (Lytton) was recounting an occasion when he played on the far from dapper Billington a pretty awful practical joke.

It was during a performance of *The Mikado*, the scene in the second act when Ko-Ko - that is, Lytton himself - Pooh-Bah and Pitti-Sing

> "are prostrate on the floor in the presence of the Emperor. We three had to do our well known 'roll over' act in which I, like Pitti-Sing, had to bear the weight of the twenty stone of dear old Fred Billington.
>
> Well, an imp of mischief led me one night to conceal a bladder under my costume, and when Fred rolled over, it exploded with a terrible bang. Billington had the fright of his life.
>
> 'What's happened, Harry?' he whispered anxiously, his nose still to the floor. 'What have I done?' "

In relating this incident Lytton claims that what he did was a "youthful folly", and thus by implication that it had happened a long time before. Yet if that was the case, his victim was hardly likely to have been Billington but, rather, some other performer who had played Pooh-Bah, simply because Billington and he had played together in *The Mikado* only a handful of times before 1909. But he says it was Billington. It certainly sounds like Billington. And if it sounds like Billington we can surely take it that it *was* Billington.

Any mention of Henry Lytton in these years also calls for mention of a female member of the Company with whom his name will always be linked – and that of course was Bertha Lewis. Bertha Lewis had had an initial period in D'Oyly Carte between 1906 and 1910, starting as a chorister and small part player, and featuring as a chorister during part of Helen Carte's second "Revivals" season at the Savoy.

Thereafter she had briefly graduated to principal contralto, but had then left the Company and only re-joined it in December 1914. This time, however, she did so as principal contralto from the first; and this time too, as she soon made clear, she was staying for good. Formidable both on stage and off, she eventually came to be regarded as "Queen" of the Company – "Queen", that is, to match Lytton's "King".

During the war years, though, she was still in the process of working her way up to this status; and however important she was to Lytton, she was not a specially significant figure so far as Fred Billington was concerned. The reason for this had to do with the fact that the G&S heavy baritone and contralto have surprisingly little interaction on stage. In *The Mikado*, for example, Pooh-Bah has just one brief exchange with Katisha. In *The Gondoliers* Don Alhambra has an even briefer one with the Duchess of Plaza-Toro. In *The Yeomen of the Guard* Wilfred Shadbolt has no interaction with Dame Carruthers at all – and so on.

Only in *Iolanthe* as Private Willis and the Fairy Queen, and in *HMS Pinafore* as Captain Corcoran and Little Buttercup do their paths significantly cross; and Billington, as already mentioned, had now given up Private Willis and had long since given up Captain Corcoran.

But if he had little to do on stage with Bertha Lewis, it was, as always, rather different when it came to the Company soubrette. During the war years the soubrette was a young lady named Nellie Briercliffe, and she – there was no doubt about this – had a lot to live up to, both with Billington himself and the D'Oyly Carte Company as a whole.

Jessie Rose, who had previously made such an impression in the soubrette parts, had left the Company in 1909, and in the interim her place had been taken by Beatrice Boarer. Beatrice Boarer seems to have been one of the many D'Oyly Carte performers down the years who did well enough in their time though left no very deep mark once they'd gone.

But with Nellie Briercliffe it was back to the way things had been with Jessie Rose and, arguably, to an even greater extent. She, like both Jessies (Rose and Bond) was another performer who had unquestioned star quality. She was petite, perky and very pretty; and she quickly acquired an ever increasing number of male admirers. One of those admirers was none other than Rupert D'Oyly Carte, son of Richard, who had become head of the Company on the death of Helen.

In the D'Oyly Carte Archive there are three letters from Rupert Carte that relate to her early days in the Company. Two of these letters were written to Sir George Power, a tenor who, in the Company's own early days, had created the parts of Ralph Rackstraw in *HMS Pinafore* and Frederic in *The Pirates of Penzance*, and who had since become a widely respected singing teacher. "I have," began Carte in the first of these letters,

> "a very promising little girl who has just joined my Company and is taking up all the Jessie Bond parts.
>
> Her name is Nellie Briercliffe. She has had no experience of Sullivan's music, and I want someone who really understands our work to give her a few hints to put her on the right road.
>
> My Company is round London for the next month. Would you be able to give Miss Briercliffe a little time? I know that you know exactly what is wanted."

For a man as painfully shy as Rupert D'Oyly Carte was known to be, a man who rarely made a warm comment about, or personally complimented, any member of his Company, that almost fatherly phrase "a very promising little girl" was surely revealing. And his third letter, written to the "little girl" herself, was more revealing still. It was dated June 12th 1915 when she had been in the Company eight months.

"Dear Miss Briercliffe

I do not expect to see you again before the vacation, so am sending you this to congratulate you on the progress you have made [during] your first tour with us. I thought your Iolanthe [on] Thursday showed much improvement.

You have certainly worked hard for us, and we are all very pleased to have you in the Company.

I am sending you a small present towards the fees I think you told me you had to pay to your agent, but please keep this strictly to yourself, as it is quite outside the rules!

I hope you will have a good holiday."

What might he have given to be playing Wilfred Shadbolt to her Phoebe? Instead, of course, it was Fred Billington who for the moment was playing Shadbolt to her Phoebe, not to mention Pooh-Bah to her Pitti-Sing. The fact that she had, like Henry Lytton, to bear his weight on top of her in their scene with the Mikado caused at least one of her fans to wonder what this felt like each time, given how slight and slender she was herself.

Ah yes, Billington's weight. It's something that's difficult to get away from. So how much did he weigh now? Was it really twenty stone, or did Lytton when he mentioned it simply pluck that figure out of the air? A possible answer to both questions may be found in the Manchester interview Billington had given in 1913. Eighteen months previously, he had told the interviewer, he had indeed weighed twenty stone. By "a simple system of diet" he had got himself down to fifteen stone, but for all that it wasn't long before the figure had started creeping up again. Nonetheless, wrote the interviewer, "he is today in the pink of condition".

Perhaps in 1913 he was. In the pink of condition - and fat: that was undoubtedly how most of his D'Oyly Carte fans wanted him to be. His size was what defined him above all. "It would be a little tragedy if he lost weight," wrote one journalist of his performances in the years during the war. "There is mirth in girth," wrote another in the same strain.

Certainly his love of food had in no way diminished. Henry Lytton had an anecdote about that too:

"One day he invited three of us to a round of golf, and it being a cold morning he told us that he was ordering 'a good beef-steak and kidney pudding'. Well, when we had finished the game and returned to the clubhouse, in came that steaming pudding.

Billington looked at it long and earnestly. 'It won't do for four,' he reflected. Then a pause. 'It would make a poor meal for three. There's scarcely enough for two. I'll tell you what. I'll have it – and you three can have chops.'

And that is just what we did."

"It won't do for Four" (see opposite page)
(Artist: Penny Woodruff)

Yet as in the 1890s before he had his first serious illness, he was building up trouble for himself. Sometime in 1915 he apparently suffered a slight stroke and, all other factors apart, this had an instant effect on his work capability. During the second half of that year he was "off" a number of times (seventeen shows out of a possible hundred and twenty-three between July and the end of the year in which he should have appeared) including three whole weeks over the Christmas-New Year period.

Was this to be the end of his working life? For the moment the answer was "no". He was determined not to give in to his condition, to acknowledge any feeling of decline or loss of energy. Told by his doctor, first, that his heart was weak and that he should no longer dance on stage, and then being positively forbidden to do so, he had responded by sending the blameless medical man a curt note:

"Dear Doctor
    I am going to dance tomorrow night. Come and see me drop down dead on the stage.
                Yours
                  Fred Billington."

Unfortunately, if unsurprisingly, the discomforts and frustrations of all this combined to make him irascible and high-handed, and many members of the Company got on the wrong side of him as a result. Most of those who experienced his high-handedness, though, simply put up with it for the sake of peace.

But one who didn't was Dewey Gibson, then the leading principal tenor. At one theatre they were playing, Gibson decided, without asking Billington's permission, to use his dressing room as a short cut to his own room, and had just reached the door of the latter room when Billington bellowed from behind him:

"Where do you think you're going?"

Gibson turned to face him calmly.

"To my room, Billy," he said.

"Oh, are you?" countered Billington. "Well, you can think again about *that*. This is my dressing room, not a bloody right of way."

Gibson remained unmoved.

"I'm going through here," he said. "It's nearer, I have to make a quick costume change. And if you think you can intimidate me in the way you intimidate everyone else, you've made a big mistake."

When a principal performer is "off" – especially when he's off with some frequency or for any length of time – the spotlight automatically falls on his understudy. For the latter it can be a crucial period in terms of his career as a whole – a chance to show whether he can handle the responsibility involved and what he can do on his own account. Fred Billington's understudy by this time was Leo Sheffield.

PUBLISHED BY   MR. LEO. SHEFFIELD   PARKSLEE PICTURES
No. 10   (D'OYLY CARTE OPERA CO.)

Leo Sheffield
(Author's collection)

Leo Sheffield was born in 1873, which thus made him nineteen years Billington's junior. Interestingly he was also a Yorkshireman, though he hailed from Malton in the East Riding rather than Lockwood in the West. Like Billington he spent much of his boyhood singing in a church choir, in his case the prestigious choir of York Minster; and like Bertha Lewis he had had an earlier spell with D'Oyly Carte.

This had lasted from 1906 to 1909, and incorporated not just one but both of Helen Carte's Savoy "Revivals" seasons. During this spell he had played such parts as Samuel in *Pirates*, Strephon in *Iolanthe*, Luiz in *The Gondoliers* and the Lieutenant in *The Yeomen of the Guard*. No less to the point, he had been instructed how to play those parts by Gilbert himself.

He had also experienced Gilbert in the same capacity after his first spell in D'Oyly Carte, when he landed a part in the librettist's final opera, *Fallen Fairies*, an opera with music by Edward German – the curious result of all this being that he had far more first-hand experience of Gilbert in not much more than three years than Billington had had in more than thirty. There were only two possible periods in which Billington can have had such experience himself: first during his spell in *The Mikado* at the Savoy back in 1896-97, and second if - *if* - he spent time as an understudy at the same theatre in 1908. But if he did experience Gilbert in this capacity, he never seems to have spoken about it to anyone else. By contrast Leo Sheffield talked or wrote about his encounters with the librettist on any number of occasions.

On his return to the Company, first as Billington's understudy and later as his successor, Sheffield eventually played all the latter's "Barrington" parts. Another tall man, solidly built though never running to anything like Billington's excess weight, with a wonderfully rubbery face together with a voice that positively oozed humour, he was *made* to be an actor-comedian. But in certain respects his performances and Billington's may not have been all that dissimilar. He relished playing in G&S just as much as Billington did, and like him, too, conveyed to his audiences an unfailing sense of delight in what he was doing.

And guess what! He was yet another D'Oyly Carte golf fanatic.

Back to the war, and the D'Oyly Carte touring schedules.

It seems to have been the case that the Company never had seriously to revise those schedules at any stage during the conflict – with just one exception. That exception occurred at Easter 1916 and concerned a visit to Ireland.

They'd already been once to Ireland during the war. The earlier visit, in April 1915, had been unremarkable, in the sense that nothing had happened to make them feel the Irish audiences were any less enthusiastic and welcoming than they'd been on all their peacetime visits.

That year, 1916, they were due to open at the Gaiety Theatre in Dublin on Easter Monday, April 24th, all set – as the *Irish Times* put it – to once again "gladden the hearts of the numerous admirers of the Gilbert and Sullivan operas". But there would be no G&S gladdening of hearts this time.

Leo Sheffield on the golf course
(D'Oyly Carte Archive)

For in Dublin that Easter Monday there erupted the Sinn Fein Rebellion, a rebellion by Irish Home Rulers against the longstanding control of Ireland by the British.

The trouble began with a group of the rebels seizing the main post office, and before long the situation developed into what became a six day battle. On the one hand were the rebels themselves; on the other were contingents of British troops quickly deployed by the authorities to put the rebellion down. Suddenly for anyone to venture out into the streets became fraught with danger.

The members of the D'Oyly Carte Company, who had arrived in Dublin on the Sunday, were lodged in various places around the city. Billington, as usual, was ensconced in the Gresham Hotel, as was Henry Lytton; and there he stayed, becoming more and more on edge as the days went by. Before long the hotel was occupied by British soldiers and refugees from other buildings. Shutters and bedding were placed in front of windows and doors to take the force of bullets fired by rebel snipers outside. Stocks of food in the hotel, always such a crucial factor in Billington's wellbeing, got lower and lower.

But in the end even food ceased to be his main concern. It was the crack of the bullets being fired by one sniper in particular that finally got to him. And eventually there came a moment when "in utter weariness", according to Lytton - though "nervous exhaustion" might describe it better – he suddenly broke out with

"Oh Harry, I do wish that bally woodpecker would chuck it!"

though it can be taken as read that he used a stronger word than "bally"; and that it probably wasn't the only stronger word he used that week.

Because of all this the Company never made it on stage that Dublin visit even once. For whatever reason Belfast, their other regular Irish venue, was not on the schedule that year. But Cork was, and they should have moved on to Cork once the Dublin visit was over. Instead, the Cork visit was summarily cancelled. The Company's priority now was to get back to the British mainland as soon as possible; and fortunately they were able to do so before any real disaster struck them. "Am leaving for England," Bertha Lewis wrote in her diary,

"after being compelled to remain in Dublin for eight days. Never could any soul know what that means to me at this moment. Away from all the bloodshed, and, thank God, all the lives of our Company are spared."

It was an experience which she, and most of the rest of the Company, eventually got over. But it was one from which Fred Billington never fully recovered.

The Dublin Rebellion, moreover, was not the only occasion on which the Company got caught up in hostilities during the war. Much less concentrated in timescale – indeed spread over a considerable period – but no less damaging in the effect they produced were the Zeppelin raids.

The raids on British towns by Zeppelin bombers and other planes were the most obvious manifestation of the fact that the civilian population at home had been inexorably drawn into the war. They had begun in December 1914, and by the time they stopped they had left more than five and a half thousand people dead and injured. They produced a variety of reactions, including schoolboy fascination and bellicose gloating in the press whenever one was brought down.

But above all they created widespread fear and alarm, partly because aerial attack in any shape or form was something that had never been experienced before, and the more so because of the possibility that they might come – and come anywhere - at any time.

For the members of the D'Oyly Carte Company this was how, justifiably or otherwise, it began to seem. In January 1916, for example, there was a raid on Hull while they were there. The following September there was a raid on Sheffield while they were *there*. In February 1917 there was to be a raid on Wimbledon in South London while they were *there* – and so on.

And whatever their effect on the Company in general, they got right under the skin of Fred Billington. One day, again according to Henry Lytton, he burst out with the statement

"Do you know, Harry, I believe that bally Kaiser has got our tour"

meaning that he thought the Germans had somehow obtained the Company's tour schedules, and by extension that the Zeppelins were deliberately targeting D'Oyly Carte and what the Company represented as a way of damaging, or even destroying, British morale. And it's just as certain that, as in Dublin, Billington used a stronger word than "bally". That bally Kaiser, it's also worth noting, was the Wilhelm who had seen Billington play Pooh-Bah when in Berlin with the Continental companies way back in the 1880s.

Billington's particularly edgy reaction to what he called the "Zepps" can, as with his reaction to the Dublin sniper, be put down to the state of his health. That this was now fragile and anything but good there seems no doubt.

Age, too, was taking its toll. He was no longer quite the Fred Billington he had previously been. It was a phase of his life – how can one one put it sympathetically without being unnecessarily dramatic? – a phase of his life marked by an underlying sense of sadness.

"I am the Coroner", 1917

"He was steeped in Savoy traditions, and as great a stickler for precedent as Gilbert himself, and his store of reminiscences was inexhaustible. Many were included in a book written by somebody else. But he had many more. Time and again we discussed their compilation in book form, but we never got to print."

(A journalist friend, in one of Billington's obituaries)

On July 16th 1917 the Company began a new tour at the Pleasure Gardens Theatre, Folkestone. They opened with a performance of *The Gondoliers*. In that performance Don Alhambra was played by Leo Sheffield. Once again Fred Billington was off, presumably "indisposed".

During the next three months or so Billington was indisposed and unable to take his place on stage on all too many occasions. He apparently, for instance, played full weeks at Plymouth and Bristol in September. But for the larger part of October he was again missing, though now, it was reported, convalescing at Colwyn Bay in North Wales. And he didn't rejoin the Company till October 29th when they began a week's season at the New Theatre, Cambridge.

Despite the war, now grinding on towards its fourth winter, and the endless toll of death and destruction it brought with it – despite this and the fact that a great many members of the University were away in the Forces – the Cambridge audiences of the time were among the most uninhibitedly enthusiastic audiences the Company attracted anywhere. In the University (and the same, it had better be quickly said, was true of Oxford) G&S was then, to use a modern term, unashamedly "cool".

"Anything which will help people to forget, if only for a few hours, the worries of wartime is to be welcomed, and certainly there is nothing which will do this so effectually as a Gilbert and Sullivan opera," wrote a reviewer in the

Cambridge Daily News; and that week in 1917 the city's enthusiasm for G&S was higher than ever. By mid-afternoon on the Tuesday every seat in the theatre had been taken for every one of the seven performances. Never in the experience of its current manager, reported the *News*, had all the seats for *any* series of performances by anyone been sold so early. It was the first time in the experience of the box office that there had been "one unbroken rush of people for tickets from eleven o'clock in the morning till four in the afternoon".

The programme for the week comprised five different operas ("the five most popular operas", as the *News* called them) and ran as follows:

Monday:	*The Mikado*
Tuesday:	*Patience*
Wednesday:	*The Gondoliers*
Thursday:	*The Yeomen of the Guard*
Friday:	*Iolanthe*
Saturday matinee:	*The Mikado*
Saturday evening:	*The Yeomen of the Guard*

As he was no longer in *Patience* or *Iolanthe*, Billington would therefore appear in five of the seven performances – assuming, that is, that he stayed the course. And his performance on the Monday suggested he would stay the course triumphantly:

"Who that has ever seen the opera can forget the Pooh-Bah of Mr Fred Billington?" (wrote the *News* reviewer of that evening).

"Mr Billington has been nearly forty years in the service of the D'Oyly Carte Company, and has played this particular part well over three thousand five hundred times, but he makes every joke seem new. His seraphic smile is alone sufficient to drive away any fit of melancholy."

Three days later – that is, on the Thursday – he gave a performance of Wilfred Shadbolt that the paper described as "brilliant".

Thursday gave way to the Friday: Friday November 2nd.

That Friday morning Billington took a train down to London. He did this because he'd been invited out to lunch. Given his invariable reaction to the prospect of food, there was no way he was going to turn the invitation down; and that was especially the case in this instance as it had come from no less a person than Rupert D'Oyly Carte. The venue suggested by Carte was the Great Eastern Hotel by Liverpool Street Station; a hotel in which, as previously mentioned (page 36) Billington had stayed several times as a resident, the station itself being conveniently the station at which he would arrive in London that day.

The lunch itself was everything he would have wished it to be. The two of them had the lot, or so the story went, including a bottle of wine, and they finished with cigars. They talked convivially as they ate and drank. As a pair they were, it appears, on terms of friendship, even if it was a friendship nowhere near as close as Billington's friendship with Helen D'Oyly Carte had been.

The meal over, however, a certain uneasiness crept into the atmosphere. Rupert Carte had something to say to Billington that he must have suspected Billington would not want to hear. The assumption has always been – and assumption it has to be, because there was no one else privy to the conversation to confirm or dispute it – that he told him he had decided the Company's current tour would be his (Billington's) last.

Yet it's surely an assumption that is justified. And given Billington's recent health record, the decision was hardly an unreasonable one. But there seems no doubt it came to Billington as a shock.

There was nothing more to say – on either side. Carte rose from the table and left. Billington found himself chatting to one of the hotel waiters, a man he had known for some years. They reminisced about old times. Then Billington said he would leave and go and sit in the train that would take him back to Cambridge, adding sardonically, "We've had no Zepps there." He rose from the table in turn, walked down the corridor towards the hotel entrance – and dropped dead.

The event made news. "Fred Billington was dead." Wasn't he someone who people had blithely imagined would go on for ever? Dead, too, just when it seemed he had recovered his old spirits. Obituaries of him appeared in newspapers all over the country. "*Pace*, Billy, old friend!" wrote one obituarist, a journalist who had known him personally, "you died in harness. I think you would have preferred it so."

And not just in harness, but suddenly – totally suddenly too. Did he have a premonition that was the way he'd go – one day if not immediately? Was it even some form of wish-fulfilment? If he could choose how he wanted to die, he had actually told Henry Lytton, it would be to have "a good dinner, a bottle of wine, a good cigar, a good joke, and – pop off." In his autobiography Lytton claimed that Billington had come out with this statement the very night before the event. This may have been author's licence. But the point doesn't really matter one way or the other. Nothing could alter the fact that Fred Billington was now dead.

He was sixty-three.

A sudden death calls for a post-mortem and an inquest even in wartime, however ironic it may be that the thousands of soldiers killed in France and elsewhere during these years were never accorded anything remotely similar; and the inquest on Billington was held in London the following Tuesday, November 6th. A jury installed, the City Coroner, a Dr Waldo, opened the proceedings by remarking that he remembered Mr Billington as a most entertaining interpreter of Gilbert and Sullivan operas.

There were three people called to give evidence, and first of the three was Rupert D'Oyly Carte. "Mr D'Oyly Carte," ran one account of their testimonies, "said that of recent years Mr Billington had not been in good health, and had suffered from a weak heart and bronchitis. Recently he had had to give up golf, his chief recreation. He was advised by an eminent doctor to lead a very steady and careful life. He was a very great eater."

"A vegetarian?" enquired the Coroner, in all apparent innocence.

"Oh no," said Mr Carte, immediately putting him right, "he was not a vegetarian. He was a large meat eater."

Carte went on to say that Billington was "a temperate man". He mentioned his fondness, as a smoker, for heavy dark tobacco. He told the court that on the day of his death he "seemed cheerful and well"; and he was then asked by Arthur Barlow, a solicitor acting for Billington's estate, about the actor's performances in Cambridge that week. Perhaps somewhat reluctantly, Carte replied that Billington's performances that week had been "better than ever". He then explained about Billington's touring lifestyle and the fact that he had had "no fixed abode".

Carte was followed into the witness box by David Groom, the waiter with whom Billington had chatted immediately before his death. And finally it was the turn of Dr Motosran (or Motafram – the correct name could be either – or neither) the doctor who had carried out the post-mortem, and who provided the relevant medical details:

"Dr Motosran said that deceased was five foot nine inches high and weighed eighteen stone. His heart weighed twenty-six ounces, and was defective from fatty degeneration and disease of the valve and blood-vessels.

The Coroner: 'The normal weight of the heart is twelve ounces?'

Dr M: 'Yes. Too much meat would tend to cause such a state of the heart in a man who was unable to take sufficient exercise. The immediate cause of death was syncope, due to an overloaded stomach pressing upon a weak heart'."

The witness testimonies and the Coroner's summing up concluded, the jury returned a verdict of "Death from natural causes". It can hardly have been a difficult verdict to reach. As a footnote to it all, it was reported by one paper that he was found when he died to have no less than £66 on him. And it's worth a second footnote to record that it wasn't apparently mentioned anywhere, though it surely ought to have been, just how appropriate it was that he, of all D'Oyly Carte people, should have died in a hotel.

On November 12th – that is, six days after the inquest – his funeral took place at Highgate Cemetery in North London. On his coffin was a large wreath with the inscription "To dear old Billy from the D'Oyly Carte Opera Company". The mourners included two of his colleagues from many years past, Courtice Pounds and George Thorne.

His will, dated February 25th 1910, was not surprisingly a shorter one than that of Helen D'Oyly Carte. In it, having no family to consider, he left all he possessed to a lady named Eva Kate Steward. Eva Steward lived in Nottingham and was the wife of a man named Francis Joseph Steward. It can only, I suspect, be guesswork what part she had played in Billington's life. He also named her, along with Arthur Barlow, the solicitor mentioned above, as his executor.

Interestingly he described himself in his will as "Frederick Billington of the Savoy Hotel" – not a bad address for a man of "no fixed abode".

Fred Billington, doyen of the D'Oyly Carte Company, might be dead. But for the rest of the Company life had to go on – and go on straight away. In Cambridge on the Saturday, the day after his death, the audiences for the two performances found a black-edged "indulgence slip" in their programmes stating that "owing to the regrettable sudden death of Fred Billington yesterday, [his] parts will be played today by Leo Sheffield"; and from that day the latter slipped seamlessly into Billington's place as the Company's principal heavy baritone.

Billington, of course, was not easily forgotten, either by the D'Oyly Carte audiences or by the press. Here are just three of the many instances in which his name found its way into the newspapers during the long D'Oyly Carte years after his death:

"There are some of us who cannot forget George Thorne's wonderfully artistic playing of Jack Point, nor see any Wilfred Shadbolt without recalling Fred Billington."

(*Western Daily Press*, Bristol, 1919)

"Mr Sydney Granville, that excellent Savoyard, now plays what people of my generation still speak of as the Billington parts."

(*Liverpool Post* [?], 1931)

"For many years the portly figure of Fred Billington filled, in more senses than one, the heavy comedy parts such as Pooh-Bah, and was a great favourite."

(*Cork Evening Echo*, 1956)

So how shall we round things off? How shall we say goodbye to Billington and his richly colourful individualistic world? Let's go first for another of his interests in later life, an interest recorded in the obituary written by his journalist friend and one not mentioned previously in this book:

"His favourite distraction was moving pictures, with special preference for films of the Wild West variety.

'Ay, lad,' he said to me, 'I just love to see those pictures of Indians and cowboys galloping across prairies.'

124

Strange preoccupation for so genuine an artist, but there was no mistaking his enjoyment."

And second – and finally – let's return to his dressing room confrontation with Dewey Gibson, the anecdote I related on page 114. It's an anecdote that shows him in – what shall we say? – a somewhat unsympathetic light. The source of it is the autobiography of Martyn Green, the performer who eventually succeeded Henry Lytton in the Grossmith parts. Green didn't actually join D'Oyly Carte till 1922 and never met Billington, so some of the details of the story as he tells it may well be inaccurate.

But never mind.

In re-telling the story myself, however, I deliberately left out the sequel. And the sequel is important because it throws a very different light on Billington's behaviour on that occasion. So here it is now. Just as Gibson was about to go through the door into his own dressing room, Billington called him back.

"Come here!" he ordered in a thunderous roar, and Gibson turned and came.

"Damn it!" said Billington as the pair stood facing each other, now no more than inches apart. "Put it there. You're the only person who has had the guts to answer me back for years. Use the damn room as a passage any time you like, and don't bother to knock. And come and have a drink when the curtain falls."

Then having related the story, Martyn Green added a question:

"Can one help liking a man like that?"

Well – can one?

Billington (third from left) with Lytton (first on left) and two other members of
the Company
(Collection: Brian Jones)

Principal Sources Used

BOOKS

Barrington, Rutland – *Rutland Barrington ... by himself.* London, 1908, pp.38-9, 57
Cellier, Francois and Bridgeman, Cunningham – *Gilbert, Sullivan and D'Oyly Carte.* London, 1914, pp.73-4, 383-8. [This was almost certainly the book "written by somebody else" referred to in the first paragraph on page 120]
Clarke, Brian – *The History of Lockwood and North Crosland.* Lockwood, 1980
Green, Martyn – *Here's a How-de-do.* London, 1952, pp.174-7
Grossmith, George – *Piano and I: further reminiscences.* Bristol, 1910, pp.40, 50-1
Harman, Lindsay – *A Comic Opera Life.* West Hartlepool, 1924, pp.58-9
Lytton, Henry A. – *The Secrets of a Savoyard.* London, 1922, pp.66, 105-9
Thorne, George – *Jots.* Bristol, 1897, pp.74-84, 109-15

UNPUBLISHED SOURCES

Billington's will, February 25th 1910
Birth and death certificates
Census records, 1841-1901
D'Oyly Carte Archive: letters from Rupert D'Oyly Carte to Sir George Power and Nellie Briercliffe
D'Oyly Carte Letter Books: letters written by Richard and Helen D'Oyly Carte. V&A Theatre Collections
Helen D'Oyly Carte's will, March 11th 1910

BILLINGTON INTERVIEWS

"Career of Pooh-Bah". *Daily Dispatch*, Manchester, March 7th 1913

"Chat with a Celebrated Actor: Mr Fred Billington at Wolverhampton".
  Midland Counties Express, Wolverhampton, December 12th 1896, p.15
"Fred Billington: some words with a 'heavy' comedian". *Sunday Times*,
  Johannesburg, April 15th 1906, p.3
"Fred Billington talks again". *Sunday Times*, Johannesburg, April 29th 1906,
  p.3
"Pooh-Bah: a chat with Fred Billington". *Gazette and News*, Blackpool,
  September 27th 1898

THE OTHER *SUNDAY TIMES* JOHANNESBURG INTERVIEWS

"Duke of Plaza-Toro: a talk with Mr Workman". March 25th 1906, p.3
"Pacie Ripple Talks". April 22nd 1906, p.3
"Some Savoyana", by C.H. Workman. April 8th 1906, p.3
"The Vicissitudinous Career of H.E. Bellamy". May 6th 1906, p.3

SOME PRESS NOTICES

Billington as

Bill Bobstay. *Era*, September 28th 1879, p.12
Captain Corcoran. *Western Morning News*, June 20th 1882, p.2
Colonel Calverley. *Bristol Times and Mirror*, May 29th 1888, p.5
          Huddersfield Daily Chronicle, May 22nd 1888, p.3
Dick Deadeye / Dr Daly. *Bath Chronicle*, May 19th 1881
Don Alhambra. *Daily Mail*, Hull, February 20th 1900, p.4
          Western Mail, November 24th 1909, p.6
King Hildebrand. *Bristol Times and Mirror*, May 22nd 1909, p.3
Pooh-Bah. *Brighton Gazette*, July 28th 1885
          Cambridge Daily News, October 30th 1917, p.3
          Era, November 7th 1896, p.13
          Evening Express, Aberdeen, January 7th 1913
          Huddersfield Daily Chronicle, May 24th 1888, p.3
Private Willis. *Sunday Times*, Johannesburg, April 1st 1906, p.3
Rajah of Chutneypore. *Leicester Mercury*, April 12th 1892
Sergeant of Police. *Sunday Times*, Johannesburg, April 22nd 1906, p.3
          Western Morning News, February 19th 1895, p.5
Sir Despard. *Salisbury Journal*, July 16th 1887, p.8
Wilfred Shadbolt. *Daily Mail*, Hull, November 3rd 1917, p.1
          Huddersfield Daily Chronicle, October 24th 1899, p.4
          Sunday Times, Johannesburg, April 29th 1906, p.3

ARTICLES

"August 1885: the Invasion of New York", by Brian Jones; in *The Mikado: a
  booklet* ... Sir Arthur Sullivan Society, 1985, pp.21-32

"Barrington on Encores" [Jessie Rose's introduction to his O.P. Club talk].
Era, January 23rd 1909, p.15

"The Curious Tale of Pacie Ripple", by Michael Walters; in *Palace Peeper*,
New York, May 1992, pp.5-7

"D'Oyly Carte and the Pirates", by Colin Prestige; in *Gilbert and Sullivan:
papers presented at the International Conference* ... University of
Kansas Libraries, 1971, pp.130-42

[George Thorne's Marriage]. *Era*, October 20th 1883, p.8

[Rutland Barrington as Dr Daly]. *Era*, December 9th 1877, p.12

SOME OF BILLINGTON'S OBITUARIES

Cambridge Daily News, November 3rd 1917, p.4
Daily Mail, November 3rd 1917, p.5
Daily Mail, Hull, November 3rd 1917, p.1
Daily Sketch, November 3rd 1917
Huddersfield Daily Examiner, November 5th 1917, p.4
"A Loss to the stage", by Bayard. Unidentified source, November 4th 1917
Sheffield Daily Telegraph, November 5th 1917, p.6

THE INQUEST

Cambridge Daily News, November 7th 1917, p.4
Westminster Gazette, November 6th 1917, p.6

Index

(Figures in bold type indicate illustrations)

Billington, Fred (cont)
  ship's concert, 43
  smoking, 37, 123
  South Africa, interest in, 99, 104
  South Africa, tour of, 87-8, **89**, 90, 92, 94, 96, 99
  stardom, 25, 76, 87-8, 91, 100, **102**
  touring, general, 16, 32-3, 66, 76
  weight, 36-7, 67, 75, 88, 110, 112, 116, 123
  will, 124
  Yorkshire origins and characteristics, 2-4, 7, 11, 13, 35, 72, 76-8, 88, 90, 92, 116
Billington, George [brother], 9
Billington, James [hangman], 39
Billington, Joseph [brother], 9
Billington, Sarah [mother], 8-9, 38
Billington, Thomas [father], 8-9, 38
Billington, Walter [brother], 9, 37-8
Billington, W.O. [cricketer], 37-9
Birmingham, 16
Bishopsgate [London], 14, 16
Black, Broughton, 58
Blackpool, 77
Bloemfontein, 87, 96, 98
Boarer, Beatrice, **102**, 111
Bond, Jessie, 22, **61**, 70, 94-5, 111
Bonsall, Bessie, 70
Bootle, 91
Bosworth, John, 48
Bournemouth, 83
Bradberry, C.H., **102**
Bradford, 60
Braham, Carrie, 12
Braham, Leonora, 64
Breslau, 48
Briercliffe, Nellie, 111-12
Brighton, 30, 42, 46, 71
Bristol, 28, 30, 59, 100, 120, 124
Brook, Herbert, **17**
Browne, George Byron, 46
Budapest, 49
Buenos Aires, 91
Bury, **34**, 35
Buxton, 33

Caddy, Miss T.; see Forster, Kate
Cadwaladr, Lyn, **17**, 60
Cambridge, 16, 107, 120-4

Fisher, David, 49, 52, 60
Fitzalmont, 14, **15**
Flushing, 48
Folkestone, 35, 80-1, 84, 120
Forster, Kate, 41, 43-4, 46, 50, 52, 54, **55**, 67, 94
Friedrich, Kaiser, 57

Gardiner, Evelyn, 4
George, Ethel, **102**
George V, King, 101
German, Edward, 116
Gibson, Dewey, 114, 125
Gilbert, W.S., 12, 14, **15**, 16, **17**, 20, 22-3, 25, 41-2, 48, 58, 60, 71, 77-9, 107, 116, 120
Glasgow, 77
Godwin, A.H., 18
Gondoliers, The, 19-20, 22, 62, **63**, 64, **65**, 66, 68, 78, 95, 103, 107-8, 110, 116, 120-1
Gordon, Duglas [Miss], 14
Gordon, J.M., **102**
Goulding, Charles, 4
Graham, Bruce, 5, **10**
Grand Duke, The, 19, 25, 70-1, 78
Granville, Sydney, **102**, 124
Green, Martyn, 125
Gresham, Thomas, 35
Gridley, Lawrence, 81-3
Groom, David, 122-3
Grossmith, George, 22-5, 33, 37, 60, 68-9, 73, 80, 91-2, 107, 125

Hamburg, 48
Hanley, 35
Harman, Lindsay, 36
Harrison, Fanny, **17**, 64
Harrison, George, 9
Hastings, 81, 83-4
Herbert, Henry, **102**
Herd, Sandy, 75
Hereford, 16
Hervey, Rose, 67
Hewson, Jones, 70, 84-5
Highgate [London], 123
His Majesty, 73, **74**, 75, 80, 84
HMS Pinafore, 4, 13-14, **15**, 16-18, 23-4, 27-8, 30-2, 54, 56, 59, 64, 66, 94, 101, 103, 111
Honley, 9
Hood, Basil, 78

Horner, Ralph, **17**
Howell, Minnie, **102**
Hoylake, 7
Huddersfield, 2, 8-9, 28, 38, 59, 66, 78, 88, 101
Hull, 54, 62, 64, 78, 82, 119
Hurley, Fred; see Thorne, George
Hutton, Mr, 8
Hutton, Mrs, 8

Imano, Henry M., 56, 59
Iolanthe, 19, 23, 28, 30, 32, 66, 91, 96, 101, 103, 111-12, 116, 121
Isle of Man, 27, 33

James, Albert, **102**
James, Mrs, **39**
Johannesburg, 87-8, 90-2, 94, 96, 98-9

Kimberley, 87

Lackner, G.J., **17**
Le Breton, Henry, 82
Le Hay, John, **17**
Lee, Esme, 31
Leicester, 33, 56, 67-9
Leipold, H., **15**
Leipzig, 49
Lenoir, Helen; see D'Oyly Carte, Helen
Lewis, Bertha, 110-11, 116, 118
Liverpool, 27, 31, 40, 42-3, 48, 60, 124
Liverpool Street Station [London], 36, 121-2
Lockwood, 8-9, **10**, 11, 35, 116
London, 11-12, 16, 22-3, 27, 30, 32, 35, 41, 44, 46, 52, 64, 68, 70, 76-7, 79-80,
    85-7, 90, 92, 103-4, 107, 111, 119, 121-3
Love Test, The, 14, 30
Lytton, Henry, 25, 73, 91, **102**, 106, 108, **109,** 110, 112, **113**, 118-19, 122, 125,
    126

Malton, 116
Manchester, 8, 35, 48, 59, 68, 99, 112
Mansfield, Richard, **17**
Marler, George, 30
May, Alice, 12
May, Marian, **17**
Meade, James A., 14, **15**
Merivale, Clara, 49, 52
Mikado, The, **iv,** 19-20, 23-4, 30, 36, 40-1, 43-4, **45**, 46, **47**, 48-52, 54, 56-7,

Redford, Robert, 82
Rene, Louie, **102**
Rich, Mary, 35
Richards, Arthur, 3
Rip Van Winkle, 31
Ripple, Pacie, 90-1, 98
Rome, 85
Rose, Jessie, 94-6, **97**, 98, 111
Rose of Persia, The, 78
Royal Park Theatre [London], **15**, 16
Ruddigore, 19, 22-3, 25, 52, **53**, 54, **55**, 56, 64, 68-9, 78

St Maur, Geraldine, 50
Salisbury, 54
Sandford, Kenneth, 3, 25
Savoy Hotel [London], 85, 104, 124
Savoy Theatre [London], 20, 41, 44, 52, 54, 60, 64, 67, 69-73, 76, 78-9, 84-6,
    94-5, 103-4, 110, 116
Scanlan, James, 36
Sheffield, 28, 78, 100, 119
Sheffield, Leo, 3-4, 114, **115**, 116, **117**, 120, 124
Shrewsbury, 16
Six-and-Six, 30-1
Snyder, Leonore, **65**
Sorcerer, The, 12-14, 18-19, 22-3, 27, **29**, 31, 43, 66, 87, 107
Southampton, 104
Stetson, John, 41, 44, 46
Steward, Eva Kate, 124
Steward, Francis Joseph, 124
Steward, Frank, **102**
Stockton-on-Tees, 9
Stuttgart, 49
Sullivan, Arthur, 12, **15**, 16, **17**, 20, 22-3, 41, 48, 50, 71, 77-9, 107, 111
Symes, Michael, 1

Temple, George, 14, **15**, 54, 64
Temple, Richard, 30, 59, 64
Thompson [Thorne], Geraldine, 69, 82
Thorne, George, 41-4, **45**, 46, 49, 52, 67-9, 82-3, 87, 91-2, 101, 110, 123-4
Tokyo, 92
Torquay, 16, 84
Trebizonde, The Princess of; see *Princess of Trebizonde, The*
Trial by Jury, 13, 18, 30, 48, 56-7, 66, 78, 87
Tunks, Leicester, **102**, 108
Turner, Olive, **102**

Ulmar, Geraldine, 44, 49, 52
Utopia Limited, 19, 25, 78

Vardon, Harry, 75
Victoria, Queen, 20, 67
Vienna, 49-51

Waldo, Dr, 122-3
Walker, Richard, 3
Watson, Richard, 3
Wilhelm, Kaiser, 57, 119
Williamson, Audrey, 62
Wimbledon [London], 119
Winckworth, William, 72
Windsor Castle, 20, 67
Wolverhampton, 76-7
Worcester, 16
Workman, C[harles] H[erbert], 73, 91-2, **93**, 94, 96, 98, 103, 108, 110

Yeomen of the Guard, The, 19, 22-3, 59-60, **61**, 62, 66, 68, 73, 75, 96, 99, 103, 111, 116, 121
York, 60, 116